POX BRITANNICA

POX

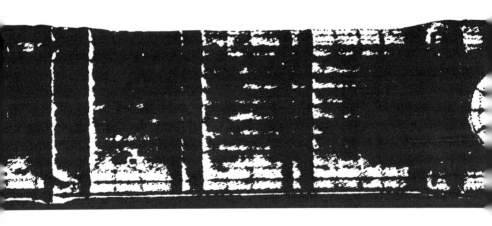

NEW YORK

BRITANNICA

THE UNMAKING OF THE BRITISH

CLIVE IRVING

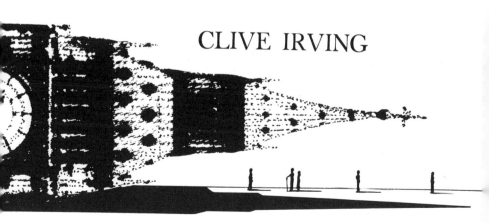

SATURDAY REVIEW PRESS | E. P. DUTTON & CO., INC.

Library of Congress Cataloging in Publication Data

Irving, Clive.
Pox Britannica; the unmaking of the British.

1. Great Britain—Economic conditions—1945–
2. Great Britain—Social conditions—20th century.
3. Great Britain—Politics and government—1945–
I. Title.
HC256.5.I78   309.1'42'085   74-6221

First Edition
10 9 8 7 6 5 4 3 2 1

Published simultaneously in Canada by Clarke, Irwin & Company Limited,
Toronto and Vancouver
ISBN: 0-8415-0341-9
Designed by The Etheredges

CONTENTS

v

PROLOGUE

Sir Henry "Chips" Channon, an American who ingratiated himself into English society, left diaries that are unmatched in revealing the insensibility of the true snob. But some things penetrated even his blasé manner. On July 7, 1939, he noted: "I have seen much, travelled far and am accustomed to splendour, but there has never been anything like tonight." The event that moved him was a ball at Blenheim, the palace built by the first duke of Marlborough on the proceeds of military genius and British chauvinism. The scene was equal to the family legend that extended from the first duke to his later relative Winston Churchill. The palace, the terraces, and the lakes were floodlit; Tyrolean singers strolled among seven hundred guests, and the supply of champagne was unlimited. Chips summed it up enviously: "It was all of the England that is supposed to be dead but isn't."

"Après moi . . ." Spectacular spasms of escapism tend to occur on the edge of apocalypse; at the time of the Blenheim ball, World War II was less than two months away. In November, 1973, a British princess married a dragoon, and for twenty-four hours reality took a minor place in the country's news coverage. The timing was precarious. The day before, on November 13, a set of disastrous trade figures precipitated panic on the London Stock Exchange. This was the first warning of a confluence of pressures—oil embargoes and industrial disputes—which, within weeks, brought the nation to a peacetime crisis worse than most people in Britain had known in their lifetime.

But it took a long time to sink in; the carnival was reluctant to admit the crisis. At the Oxford and Cambridge university rugby football game in December the normal quota of Rolls-Royces turned up, and the usual quantities of champagne were guzzled, during what are known as normal office hours. The delay in facing facts was not really so surprising, since Edward Heath's government was steadfastly refusing to admit how bad things really were. It clung to a congenitally Panglossian view.

This response was in character not only with that government but with much of the country. Diagnoses of the crisis centered on its economic and technical components. Some were valid, if unwelcome. But much of the real cause of the British trauma is not technical but emotional. Over a wide range of its affairs the country is self-deceiving.

This book is primarily about that emotional factor, and about a state of mind that made some kind of dénouement inevitable. It might have come later, rather than sooner. It might have taken any one of a number of forms. When it did come, it was made far worse by some of the many illusions that have proved remarkably persistent in Britain. Not only political policies but the country's fundamental institutions rest on a similar capacity to defer reality. But first, before assessing these structural flaws, a substantial mythology has to be dismantled, and it is one that the British are by no means alone in being addicted to.

Tolerance and decency are deeply rooted in England, but they are not indestructible, and they have to be kept alive partly by conscious effort. If liberty means anything at all, it means the right to tell people what they do not want to hear.

—GEORGE ORWELL, PREFACE TO ANIMAL FARM

I. FALLEN IDOLS

1. THE DOCTRINES OF TRUE BRIT

Sail on, All Who Still Believe . . .

Britain is more than a country: it's an idea. For years now, long after British power evaporated, the British idea has continued to fascinate people of all nationalities and races. Even those who were once under British rule, and are of normally sound mind, are drawn to the spell of the British idea.

The idea can be all things to all men. To a democrat it represents a system that works. To a conservative it shows the value of enduring standards. To a liberal it demonstrates the ideal of social tolerance. To a revolutionary like Marx it could offer both sanctuary and the frustrating triumph of gradualism. To the scholar it possesses the springs of eternal wisdom. To the sensualist it has acquired a new promise of pleasure. To the Latin it has an enviable reserve. To the pacifist it has humanitarian restraint. To the militarist it carries numerous honors in the arts of war. To the stylist it has style. Make of it what they will, all Anglophiles share one belief in their allegiance to the British idea: it is the last civilization. Decline can be overlooked as long as virtue remains. If virtue were lost, the Anglophile's most valuable bearing would be gone: the British comparison. Every problem needs its antonym.

But many paragons are fraudulent. The British idea was always a muddle of inconsistencies, as much mystique as reality. Now what reality once existed has gone. Many will find this hard to take. If sheer belief could have kept the British idea aloft, it would have been willed immortality, a testament to the power of prayer. But, as in all affairs left to men, it was mortal.

HARD FACTS FOR THE TRUE BELIEVER

1. "THE BRITISH SYSTEM WORKS."

Nobody is sure what this system is. There is supposed to be something called "parliamentary government," in the care of the "mother of parliaments." If that is so, the old girl is senile. While members of Parliament play elaborate procedural games and taunt each other with words, the power of Parliament has been steadily subverted by a nonelected bureaucracy. Simultaneously, the concept of rule by cabinet has given way to a form of presidential rule, in which the prime minister has recruited his own staff, with a heavy elitist bias, and through which all policy decisions are predigested and fixed before they reach the cabinet. This is a version of rule by "expert." Prime ministers also cultivate their own coterie of like-minded spirits to evolve their singular philosophy for how the people shall live.

In effect, power in the country has passed into invisible hands. Any idea that the destiny of the people can be entrusted to Parliament is an offense to the expertise of the "experts" who know that they know best.

Isn't this unconstitutional? It would be, if there were a Constitution. But the British are proud that their Constitution is unwritten, which means that you can make it up as you go along. A great deal of making up has been going on, probably more than at any time in British history, and certainly more than most of the British realize.

2. "THE BRITISH HAVE A GENIUS FOR CHANGING WITHOUT SEEMING TO CHANGE."

This is true. For example, there has been a great redistribution of wealth in Britain. Instead of all the country's wealth being allowed to remain in the hands of landed aristocrats, industrial plutocrats, and financiers, some of it has been redirected into the hands of property speculators, asset strippers, and new financiers.

3. "THE WELFARE STATE TAKES GOOD CARE OF THE POOR."

The welfare state was a good idea, but somehow it got overtaken by the corporate state. The idea of the corporate state is to make everybody richer by taking money from taxes and passing it to all the businessmen who know how best to use it for the national interest. In the meantime, several million people in Britain are living at, or below, the poverty line. Two and a half million are living in houses that are forgivingly described in officialese as "unfit"—which means that they lack amenities like hot water, a bathtub, or an indoor toilet. What they don't lack is squalor. When the British businessmen have made things come right, there might be money left over to take care of such minor inconveniences.

4. "THE BRITISH HAVE THEIR PRIORITIES RIGHT."

That depends on who you are. If you are in urgent need of an airplane to fly the Atlantic in three hours at something more than the regular first-class fare, then, do they have the plane for you! On the other hand, if you think it unreasonable to spend $1.9 billion of public funds to provide such a convenience when, for the same money, you could get two new cities or several hundred hospitals and schools . . .

5. "CLASS IS NO LONGER IMPORTANT IN BRITAIN."

There are basically two kinds of school in Britain: state schools and private schools. The state schools are free, the public (private) schools require most parents to pay fees of as much as $2,500 a year. In 1971, 31.5 percent of the boys going to private schools went on to university; 5.7 percent of the boys going to state schools qualified for university. The number of children going to private schools actually went down by 2 percent between 1961 and 1971, but these schools remain the best bet for parents who want to get their children into Oxford or Cambridge. And an "Oxbridge" education remains the magic key to both a career and the subtle social network that in Britain still fixes things in its own quiet way.

6. "BRITISH JUSTICE IS THE FAIREST IN THE WORLD."

Neither British judges nor British courts must be held in contempt. Contempt of court is a serious offense. This makes commentary on the courts difficult. For example, if you happened to be the parent of a child mutilated before birth by a drug called thalidomide, and you had spent years waiting to get compensation from the company that made the drug, and a newspaper took up your case and sought to make that company feel shameful in public—where would the public interest lie? In the view of the lordships of the law, the newspaper is making a mischief. The company which made the drug, and which also happens to make a half-dozen brands of the best-known whiskeys, ought not, said the court, to be "pressured" on behalf of limbless children. Such pressure, while the company and parents deliberated, is "contempt of court." The newspaper should shut up. The children should carry on waiting for the lawyers to agree.

7. "THE BRITISH POLICEMAN IS THE FINEST
IN THE WORLD."

In 1972, among the elite of the British police at Scotland Yard, 144 officers were admitted to have been "in serious trouble." Eighty of them had "retired early." Some were trafficking in drugs, some were taking bribes, some were keeping strange company.

8. "THE BRITISH CIVIL SERVANT IS THE MOST HONEST
IN THE WORLD."

Right. But you might be forgiven for the wicked thought, after studying their record, that corruption could be more efficient and less costly than integrity. Once it passes into the hands of the British civil service, money seems to decrease markedly in value and effectiveness.

9. "THERE ARE NO SERIOUS RACIAL PROBLEMS
IN BRITAIN."

Between 1948 and 1972 about one million West Indians, Asians, and Africans came to live in Britain, their "mother" country; another half million blacks were born British. At first they were called "settlers"; then "colored"; then "immigrants"; then they were invited to go back where they came from—even those who had been born in Britain. In 1964 a Tory campaigned on the ticket "If you want a nigger neighbor, vote Labour." In 1968 the Right Honorable Enoch Powell, M.P., said that allowing in the blacks was "like a nation busily engaged in heaping up its own funeral pyre." As the man who had dared to say in public what had only been whispered in private, Powell became the overnight idol of white supremacists. While they condemned Powell, both Labour and Conservative governments tightened the screw on immigration, until by the early 1970s it had virtually dried up. By then, the blacks had taken their place in British society. At the bottom. Their company was not wanted, but their utility was undeniable. They do the jobs that whites no longer will.

10. "BRITISH INVENTIVENESS HAS INSPIRED THE WORLD."

True: the British invented the Industrial Revolution and industrial pollution, child labor, sweated labor, and concentration camps. There were also more benign inventions. But being great respecters of tradition, the British revere the old values wherever possible.

11. "SUDDENLY THE BRITISH ARE SEXY."

Not suddenly; they've just been enjoying it more—or more of them have been caught enjoying it, particularly the upper classes. The upper classes always did enjoy it, but they used not to be caught. Sex was once thought too good for the lower classes, so the upper classes imagined they had kept the secret to themselves. Sex was not, after all, as the prosecutor of Lady Chatterley had implied, something you would want your servants to read about. However, the word has got out. Given the knowledge and given the Pill, the working class are enjoying sex so much that they have had to be tartly reminded that they didn't invent it. All this has been very provocative for the Puritans, who tried to stamp it out. So did their lordships of the High Court. They had about as much chance as a snowflake in hell. And just to prove that it was democratic, a government minister who was also a lord was caught with his pants down, *à trois*, with the help of a two-way mirror. In London, the two-way mirror business is booming.

12. "THERE IS NO CORRUPTION IN BRITISH PUBLIC LIFE."

Corruption runs through all levels of British public life: it is pervasive but not normally conspicuous. There is a long-established and carefully refined way of doing it. A great deal of corruption in Britain is petty. Fifty bucks will easily buy a man. Careers have been finished by the temptations of a few bottles of whiskey, a vacation in Majorca, a swimming pool in the yard. There's a subtle, interlocking brotherhood with connections in every town—and there's always the man to see. Two things enable this system to flourish: its enormous discretion, and the absence of any tradition of muckraking. When the muck does get raked, very rarely and usually by accident, there is a general howl in the land. In such bouts of self-righteousness a handful of fall guys are pilloried, usually the small fry, and many fine words spoken about the exception proving the rule. Don't you believe it.

13. "MADE IN BRITAIN MEANS MADE BY CRAFTSMEN, WITH LOVE."

There is more craftiness than craft. Nobody has turned anachronism to advantage like the British. Look at our castles, they say, and then they add: our cars are built like that. But, with some rare exceptions, that so-called hand-crafted car comes off a production line just like any other, except that the factory is probably older than most. A sleek line and a good paint job can still conceal a lot of trouble, and often does. In a world where almost anything falls to bits, the British want you to believe that their stuff won't. Why should they be so lucky? It's what's known as John Bullshit.

14. "THE BRITISH ARE KIND TO ANIMALS, CHILDREN, AND ANYONE IN NEED; THEIR WORD IS THEIR BOND; THEY HONOR GOD AND FOLLOW HIS WORD; THEY . . ."

But enough. If the True Believer has come thus far, he will want evidence. These are serious charges; idols cannot lightly be tarnished. The last people to give up the British idea will be the British themselves. There is a certain justice in this. The less real the idea gets to everybody else, the more the British hang on to it. It is a collective hallucination, remarkably durable. This state of mind shall be known as True Brit.

The essence of True Brit is a belief in greatness. More than that, it is to believe that when God was hurriedly making the world, he gave greatness to the British. In abundance. Other countries are not immune to the greatness bug, although it expresses itself differently. In America it's a question of quantity; in France, a question of style; in Russia, a question of sheer weight. To the British it's a question of quality. They have it, you don't. True Brit is taken in with the mother's milk. And if it isn't, a British education will rectify the error.

Until not so long ago the teaching of history in British schools revolved in red on a globe of the world: the stain of empire on which the sun never set. With that gone, there is plenty of greatness left. British history is presented in school as a perpetual rerun of fables, lies, and prudent editing. Defeats are allowed as a fleeting counterpoint before the next trumpet blast. Sometimes defeat is transmuted into victory, as with Dunkirk. History is an anthem, and True Brit is its beat:

True Brit,
Brit is true,
Believe in Brit,
And it comes true. . . .

The greatness of True Brit has two threads: military power and economic power. Both are sanitized like things used in saintly missions. In this respect, True Brit does less than justice to the British. The emphasis on martial clout makes muscle more important than mind. Here's a typical evocation of True Brit, published in the London *Times* as Britain joined the European Common Market:

> We are still capable of speaking about "us" and "our nation" and know what we mean. There is succour there from our inherited characteristics, our shared heroes, our victories and even our defeats. Drake, Wellington, Churchill. The defeat of the Armada. Waterloo, Dunkirk. Shakespeare, Dickens, Hardy. Our sense of fair play, and a very high grade of humour, law, government, horticulture and breakfast.

Horticulture and breakfast?

But note that Wellington gets a higher billing than Shakespeare and that Newton gets none at all. The really civilizing British ideas were secondary to the bogus Bible-thumping that went with colonial aggression. It was not the British culture that "civilized" the primitives, but the British boot and the British gun. True Brit appeals to the philistine, not the aesthete.

True Brit fosters three kinds of myth: institutional, personal, and symbolic. The institutional myths enable the British to feel that they enjoy an immunity to social instability—British law, Parliament, and even the police are inviolate. The personal myths are, except for the monarchy, all in the past. The most recent is Churchill, still a deity. A personal myth like Churchill extends to some of the symbolic myths. John Bull, so readily evoked by Churchill, began his career as a curious blend of squire and rustic, a symbol of pugnacity and probity. Later he became a chauvinist. Sometimes symbolic myths become quasi-institutional, like Rolls-Royce, which transcends prosaic engineering and, to the patriot, is shorthand for excellence. The Bank of England is not just the national treasury but a symbol of native integrity and solvency. All these myths, so embedded in True Brit, seemed as secure as they were indispensable. All have turned out to be founded on sand. Nonetheless—and this is a mark of the dependency they induce—all are desperately sustained beyond their natural life-span.

This might seem merely an unusually narcotic form of patriotism. True Brit does, indeed, exploit patriotism. But it is a kind of patriotism that begins where legitimate patriotism ends: it exists in a time warp of its own making in which the past is prolonged and reality is indefinitely deferred. It is more than jingoism, more than "my country, right or wrong." It is a system, and a system organized on the principle of self-perpetuation. But because, to retain its hold, it must set objectives that cannot in reality be met, it is also continually self-defeating.

It would be neat if True Brit could be defined as an affliction confined to one clearly motivated group or class. It would be neat, and it would be wrong. An eerie quality of True Brit is the way that it seems to occur in the most unlikely places; seemingly inexplicable behavior becomes distressingly explicable once True Brit is diagnosed. Few remain uncontaminated; it spreads easily and on contact.

In British politics, True Brit runs the whole gamut, from the supposedly far Left, through the center, and all the way out to the lunatic Right. For example, in a Socialist it expresses itself in sentimentality and nostalgia, a love for the regalia of imperialism and a mean-minded kind of isolationism. In the new Conservative revisionists it is totally without sentiment and, instead, surfaces as an indelibly bureaucratic urge to create totems of technology. On the right wing it appears as a revivalist movement, often with fire-and-brimstone-style rhetoric. It is a diversity of figures and positions with one delusion in common.

Although British blood is polyglot, True Brit would have you believe that there is an Anglo-Saxon racial purity dating from the moment when that extra share of greatness arrived in the British Isles as a divine gift. Racial mythology is the most perverted streak in True Brit, the festering resentment of the dispossessed. The British are more prone to ethnic arrogance now than ever before, both as the rationale for their racism and as the engine of their imagined esteem.

The hubris of True Brit is sustained partly by the universal admiration society that has been weaned on the British idea. If the British themselves ever have a fleeting doubt about their distinctions, there is always an Anglophile at hand to reassure them. The admirers of the British are endlessly forgiving and, it may seem, congenitally myopic. Even those harsher judges who know true decadence when they see it often still harbor a twinge of mercy, a grudging acknowledgment of some rare virtue. But they, at least, know that the game is coming to its end; the pageant is crumbling.

2. THE PAUPERS OF EUROPE

The British woke up one morning and found themselves the paupers of Europe. The most galling thing about this was the prosperity of the French and the Germans. The average British view of a Frenchman is of either a garlic-chewing peasant laboring in feudal backwaters or a perfumed adulterer indulging his *cinq à sept*. About the German he feels even less warm.

In 1958 the French gross national product was 25 percent below the British; it is now more than 25 percent ahead of it. Measured by personal income, the most prosperous part of Britain, the southeast, is equal to the poorest part of France, the southwest. Parisians are markedly richer than Londoners. Most of Britain is poorer than many European countries except middle and southern Italy and a part of Belgium. Germany is the richest of all, overtaking even the United States for the first time in 1973. In world rank, Britain is sixth, exactly half as wealthy as Germany.

What is worse, Dr. Hermann Kahn's crystal ball predicts that by 1985 Britain will be in ninth or tenth place in Europe, lagging behind Spain, Austria, and Greece. The richest will be France, outstripped in the world only by the United States and Japan. Admittedly, this humiliating prognosis was commissioned from Dr. Kahn by the French government, conveniently just before an election. Asked for a less statistical and more psychological explanation for British collapse, Kahn says, "In Britain more than anywhere else there is respect for old wealth but hostility to new wealth. The difference is that with new wealth and rapid growth the rich get richer and the poor get richer too. With slow growth like yours, the rich get richer and the poor get poorer."

In fact, social wealth and corporate wealth in Britain are in stark contrast. British companies are by far the most profitable in Europe: sixty-three of the top one hundred European companies on 1971 profit performance were British, only thirteen were German, and seven French. Kahn's thesis of polarized rather than evenly distributed wealth is valid. Britain has the most innately unbalanced society in Europe.

There is no mystery about where those company profits go: to the richest minority. Ninety-five percent of privately controlled shares in Britain are owned by 5 percent of the population, and this top 5 percent own more than half of the personal wealth of the country. The inequality of wealth in Britain is much more marked than in the United States, where the top 1 percent own 24 percent of the wealth, compared to 40 percent for the top 1 percent in Britain.

Just how rich the richest are is hard to tell, because wealth in Britain is not brandished. It reposes discreetly away from vulgar view in large estates sculptured by generations of landscape gardeners. By far the most consistent movement of wealth is not from rich to poor but from one generation of the rich to another. Even to talk of a "top 5 percent" is imprecise and misleading. The summit is reached by few; the top 5 percent includes in its bottom reaches private savings as modest as $22,500. Since the wealthy are also those who benefit most from inflation, the wave of new fortunes made in Britain on land or property has, if anything, increased the inequities.

When it reaches such proportions, the lopsidedness of society has insidious chain reactions. The poorest in Britain have the worst diets: they buy 13 percent less milk than average, 16 percent less meat, 5 percent fewer eggs. In turn, the weakness and deficiencies of diet increase the incidence of sickness, and yet the National Health Service spends one-third more on treatment for the richest than for the poorest.

Public housing subsidizes a working-class family's rent to an average of $45 a year, but the tax relief on loans for those able to buy their own homes runs at an average of $153 a year. Because their children stay at school longer and have more chance of reaching college, a family making $10,000 a year can reckon to cost the state half as much again for education as the national average. Even then, only one in eight of British children between the ages of twenty and twenty-four are in college. The welfare state has been warped so that it reflects and supports the bias in favor of rich against poor. In Britain over the few years between the mid-sixties and early seventies, about one hundred people made as much money on property speculation as it would take the average worker two thousand years to earn.

There is no discernible sense of outrage. Things have been run this way for so long that the poor are as fatalistic as the rich are intransigent. In all the other industrial democracies, the original lucre of capitalism has been ground into dust and dispersed (save, of course, for the more resilient dynasties) to the point where in, for example, the United States and France and Germany, middle-class wealth represents social equilibrium. This has happened, to the chagrin of Marxists, without requiring the dissolution of capitalism. In Britain, in the most sustained act of deception and organized cupidity since Carthage, the fruits due to the many have been retained by the few.

A curious quirk of the British psyche is that, instead of being provoked to fury by the continued injustices of their system, the people direct their resentments anywhere but at that system. Perhaps this is why the system has survived for so long—by providing decoys. As they sink into the trance of True Brit, the British seem to think that the cause of their hard times lies somewhere else, probably with foreigners. The fusion in the British soul of pride of heritage, ethnic hauteur, sanctimony, and totem worship easily turns into a sour resentment of old enemies and newly risen competitors.

Joining the European Common Market has increased rather than diminished these tensions. Forcing the British into Europe was, in any case, an act of desperation. For more than ten years, three British prime ministers tried to recover from an early blunder, when Anglo-Saxon condescension spurned invitations to sign the Treaty of Rome on the formation of the Common Market. Later, the idealism of a united Europe took on for the British a more urgent and expedient purpose. To Britain, with its economy permanently convalescent, the pound sterling ebbing away, and industrial unrest endemic, Europe seemed to offer a Draconian remedy—disciplines that couldn't be imposed from the inside would be inescapable with the country opened up to full-blooded competition.

This has never been conceded as a motive, but it had

compulsive attraction for impotent politicians. There was no other trick left to try—unless, of course, they did something about the basic inequities of wealth that were as responsible as anything for the economic shambles. But that is unthinkable.

To the rest of Europe, the British look like somebody staggering home, slightly tipsy, from a fancy-dress ball, still absurdly costumed and in the mind still living the part. As this bizarre figure knocked on the door to beg admittance, it blinked in the unwelcome light of reality and turned surly and regretful that the dream was ended. Strutting, posing and posturing, vain and patronizing, the apparition has the brittle charm of a Shakespearian fool—sometimes to be pitied, sometimes exasperating, occasionally droll. Britain is a victim of the time warp, promising to reform but really not grasping either the extent of its waywardness or the means of curing it.

The British advocates of the new Europe have tried to make up for the revolution that Britain never had. The gift of gradualism, so frequently paraded as the anchor of the country's stability, has really been its undoing. Although it is the last kind of lesson the British are ready to learn, the clue to the real cause of their strangled society lies in the fields of France. France was shaped (or rather not shaped) by the French Revolution; Britain has been shaped, in both the physical and social sense, by the Industrial Revolution.

The British conception of France as a nation of blue-smocked peasants has at one and the same time seen the point and missed it. France's industrialization was not at the expense of the peasantry (although this is beginning to change): the rural communities of France stayed in possession of their land. Wealth in land, wealth from industry, the wealth of the *rentier* in the towns, and finally the affluence of the new middle class progressed in parallel in France without any one of these groups having to give way to another. In the end this has built a spread of prosperity in significant contrast to the polarized wealth of the British.

British capitalism and the Industrial Revolution did not coincide. The pocketing of wealth by the few had already taken place before the first mechanized spinning wheel marked the end of cottage industries and the dawn of mass production. It was the venality of the Tudor monarchy that set the pattern for stripping the country of its wealth. In the reign of Henry VIII, the families from the British shires who schemed in the royal court were grabbing thousands of acres of land. More than a quarter of England was in the hands of a new landowning aristocracy. Another quarter, perhaps more, was in the hands of the Catholic Church, as much a political and capitalist enterprise as a spiritual one. The Church also collected 30 percent of the customary dues paid by smaller landowners to the greater.

With the crown increasingly desperate for money to raise armies and to defend itself, it turned on the Church and gave dispensation to the landowners to grab Church lands. By the early seventeenth century more than half of the land was in the hands of a powerful oligarchy of plundering landowners. The monarchy itself was impoverished, already decaying into a symbol and tool. The people of England had been dispossessed of what was then the only universal prospect of wealth and security: land and property.

In 1705, Thomas Newcomen built his steam engine. In 1764, James Hargreaves produced the spinning jenny, and in 1765, James Watt his condenser patent. Iron ore had been smelted by coke. All these innovations needed capital: the source of capital lay with the landowning oligarchy, families whose wealth was less than a century old. During that decisive first impact of Future Shock, there were incredible tides running: the English peasantry were coerced into industrial slavery; technology was the new witchcraft; Adam Smith wrote *The Wealth of Nations*. And the British were defeated in the American Revolution.

The world changed, but not the inherent imbalance of wealth in Britain. No wonder the British ruling classes abhorred the French Revolution and reviled Bonaparte. An alternative idea was planted in Europe, and although it took nearly two hundred years to do so, it has led finally to the humiliation of the British: an economic humiliation rather than a military one.

Now, in their ethnocentricity, the British suspect that European membership is the beginning of racial pollution, a subtler variety than they had already been asked to endure by living alongside their black slaves. One survey of British attitudes toward Europe turned up a pronounced aversion to the bidet, which is thought of as "dirty" and "Continental." Although the British are reticent on the subject, it appears that the average Briton takes a bath only once every three days.

In the British view of Europe, food seems crucial. The liberal middle class, who are mostly pro-European, have tasted French food and can't wait to see the grisly diet of the British pub replaced by the delights of the Paris bistro. The conservative working class, on the other hand, who are heavily anti-European, are deeply suspicious of anything other than their own bland and greasy diet.

A year after the British had, in theory, become fully paid-up Europeans, they were more hostile to the idea rather than less. Ironically, the greatest suspicion of and hostility toward Europeans comes from the poorest and the oldest. They do not seem to realize that of all the European democracies, the one that screws them the most is their own. It is not the Common Market that made the British the paupers of Europe.

3. IMAGES OF ALBION

It Ain't What You See, It's the Way That You See It.

Mr. Hughes looks on Britain as an English-speaking country with good communications, relatively free of bureaucracy, and somewhere that will afford him privacy.
—ANONYMOUS SPOKESMAN FOR HOWARD HUGHES

Having been dislodged by an earthquake in Central America, and fast running out of sympathetic accommodations, the millionaire settled into a floor at the Inn on the Park in London. The demands of a recluse are peculiar but not extensive. A darkened room in Mayfair is much like a darkened room anywhere. But that capsule summary of the British virtues, although a trifle expedient, did make people feel that the place still had something to offer for the more fastidious tastes. There are some people, though, for whom there can be too much civilization. S. J. Perelman, for example:

> English life, while very pleasant, is rather bland. I expected kindness and gentility and I found it, but there is such a thing as too much couth.

This was disappointing. As a lifelong Anglophile, Perelman had sold his house in New York State, spat on New York City as a pestilence to be discarded, and set out to do everything required to be an English gentleman. He had even joined the Reform Club. A year later, he was back in the most depraved quarter of New York City, seeking out his old delicatessen. Apart from being too bland, London had not been able to provide rolls with sesame seeds.

Like many another Anglophile, Perelman had been chasing moonbeams. The England he imagined, and the one he had so affectionately created in short stories, had never really existed. Phileas Fogg had never belonged to the Reform Club; he had been invented by a Frenchman. A man who behaved like Fogg would never be allowed in the company of gentlemen. He was not bland enough.

> Englishmen in Knightsbridge today stuck to their stiff-upper-lip tradition. When they saw a young man running naked down the pavement and across the busy road they averted their eyes. The man, aged about 30, was completely starkers, but he barely [sic] raised an eyebrow from many early morning shoppers and businessmen. It was only when a motor-cycle policeman stopped that a crowd began to stare. The policeman chased the naked man across the road and finally caught him on the corner of Knightsbridge and Sloane Street. A raincoat was hastily thrown over him as he lay on the pavement.
> —ITEM IN THE LONDON *Evening Standard*

Averting the gaze from the naked truth sounds amusing enough in this context, but, as Perelman said, you can have such a thing as too much couth. One of the reasons why commercial, political, and social dirty tricks pass undetected in Britain is that it is thought to be unseemly to look for them. A great deal of reliance can be placed on this fine sensibility by people who lack scruple but share, for obvious reasons, the code of discretion. Such cool makes the British feel superior:

> Naturally the British do not, among the nations, have a monopoly of good manners; but they are bringing a valuable asset to add to the existing stock of European codes of conduct.
>
> —THE LONDON *Sunday Times*

It is doubtful whether the Europeans share this euphoric view of the more abstract qualities that the British take with them as they join the Common Market. Within months of their admittance, a BBC correspondent reported that, having thought the phrase "perfidious Albion" might now be buried forever, he had heard or read it three or four times in the past three months. Furthermore, the British delegation had been, he said, falling rather short of that "existing stock of European codes of conduct"—"their behavior at the European Parliament has been described to me as that of 'men discovering with delight that Britain's Indian Empire never really died.' "

Even before the British proconsuls had crossed the Channel, a survey conducted by the scholarly British journal *New Society* turned up a surprising quirk of national racial prejudice:

> It showed how, even among people who said they were pro-Marketeers, there was much more human sympathy with the Americans (or with Nigerians) than with the French.

British reserves of "human sympathy" are, in any case, carefully conserved. They were never generous. The Americans and the Nigerians can consider themselves especially favored. As for the French, well, they would certainly return the compliment. It is hard to love a country that has twice in one century had to help save you from the Germans—and from yourselves. Building an affection for the English, if you aren't a natural Anglophile, is difficult for anybody, as the author and critic Anthony Burgess confessed:

> The impossibility of anybody's really liking the English (or, by colonial extension, the Americans either) is demonstrated again and again. The world's hope for the English, if it has one, certainly the Englishman's hope for himself, if he has one, lies in that old eagerness to teach, which, perhaps by definition, has nothing to do with being simpatico.

Well, nobody likes or loves a pedagogue, least of all a British pedagogue. But what is it that the British have left to teach other people? Integrity, perhaps?

> Only one leading democracy, Britain, has remained comparatively unspotted. The famous Profumo affair, a few years ago, astounded the British not because it disclosed a gaudy private life in higher political echelons but because a junior minister lied to the House of Commons.
>
> —C. L. SULZBERGER, *International Herald Tribune.*

Not so, and no marks for prescience: not long after this fashionable wisdom was penned, Lord Lambton followed Profumo into malodor for the same taste in private pleasure, give or take an extra partner, and although he confessed with celerity he was summarily dispatched. The real offense was screwing beneath his station. No lady arranges for photos to be taken through a two-way mirror. It was no use Lambton saying that he did it for "variety." He was slumming, and that one simply must not do.

And another thing. That spotless democracy of Cyrus Sulzberger's—so indispensable to the editorial writers of *The New York Times* every time they want to cast a shadow over their own system—is an illusion. In Britain, minor-league corruption is passed off by using the quaint term "fiddling." But attitudes toward "fiddling" are complicated by that other British vice, class prejudice. As the BBC magazine *The Listener* recorded:

> According to an anthropologist, Gerald Mars, waiters, fairground workers, dustmen, dockers and many another proletarian Uncle Tom Cobley are on the fiddle: it's often thought a legitimate part of their pay. But the middle classes fiddle too, though they look on working-class fiddles with horror.

Fiddling is nourished in the favorable, secretive climate of local government; in effect, local politics has become big business, with 16 percent of the British gross national product flowing through the hands of councils. An ex-mayor of the Yorkshire town of Pontefract, jailed in a case involving $23,500 in bribes paid to secure building contracts, said that kickbacks were the "normal run of the mill." And that, as the judge observed, seemed to be only the tip of the iceberg. But the Anglophiles of *The New York Times* will have none of it. The more depraved their own political system has become, the more dependent they are on the preservation of British virginity. The paper's most addicted upholder of British virtue, Anthony Lewis, considered the political crime of Watergate to be beyond British comprehension:

> Misuse of power on so enormous a scale is simply unimaginable here. Because they do not appreciate the occasion for it, some Britons cannot understand the public method of the Senate committee's proceedings. The correctives here are quiet and internal.

Which was, though he appeared not to know it, another way of saying that in Britain the cover-up is a tidy and highly refined art. Under the law of contempt of court, as soon as the smallest fish is caught, all the fat cats who feed off him are assured that reporters will be silenced. Sacrificial offerings are made of those dumb enough to be caught, while the rest who know better the rules of the game lie low until it is safe to play again. There may well be a difference of degree between British and American fiddling, but the corruption of ethic is identical.

And even the most hallowed symbols of patriotism are not immune to it: the Royal Navy, bulwark of Britannia, was caught with its hand in the cashbox. Seventy-five naval officers and enlisted men were convicted of kickbacks paid by firms supplying food to navy messes. Although a swindle costing $275,000 was nailed, the police estimated that the real sum had been more like $1.25 million—"this type of crime in the navy stretches back over years and years, and the total stolen must run into millions of pounds," said a detective. Time after time that ubiquitous phrase "the tip of the iceberg" was used. The truth is that British cool keeps icebergs well under the waves.

Anglophiles serve only to keep the British firm in their hypocrisy. The incorrigible Anthony Lewis again:

> Americans especially notice the difference [in Britain] from their own Galbraithian balance of private affluence and public squalor.

Which sat awkwardly in contrast to this:

> Three hundred people may die from cold on Christmas Day in Britain, the Young Liberals declared yesterday. The movement was launching a campaign to focus public attention on hypothermia, the hidden killer.
> —ITEM IN THE LONDON *Times*

During that season of good cheer, one old woman had been found dead in her home after eating cardboard in an effort to keep warm. An organization called Age

Concern was formed to provide a voluntary emergency service. In London a quarter of the houses are literally decaying; nearly two-thirds were built before the end of World War I.

But not even bombers could shake Lewis from his reverie. On the day that IRA bombs killed one man and injured two hundred people in central London, he was walking along the Thames Embankment filled with the joys of spring, and a good lunch:

> Exquisite crocuses were in bloom, yellow and purple and white. A country that still cares about flowers, I thought. . . .

In the country that still cares about flowers, the government subsidizes mining companies to drill for minerals in the national parks; resort towns discharge sewage into the ocean; remote islands that resisted two hundred years of industrialization are being appropriated for oil refineries; unpoliced factories pour sulfur dioxide into the air and lethal chemicals into the rivers.

But to be fair to Anthony Lewis, he was writing for a newspaper that has always been incorrigibly under the British spell. Clifton Daniel, that elegant courtier of the Sulzbergers at *The New York Times,* was house-trained in London society during World War II. The war that Ed Murrow reported breathlessly from the rooftops during the blitz made London for many American correspondents a curious combination of front-line action and old-world breeding. Daniel became a darling of the salons of Noel Coward, Bea Lillie, and Clarissa Spencer-Churchill and the companion of Lady Jersey, an ex-wife of Cary Grant. From then on, his suits, his patina, and even his accent were London-tailored. Such an attachment fixes a man's vision for life and easily tends to influence his work. Even Hemingway, no Anglophile and certainly not a *saloniste,* lapsed into sentiment in his London dispatches. Among other members of that American press corps in London during the war were Walter Cronkite and Drew Middleton.

The impact of that time and place on American journalism was much like the impact of a particularly engaging affair: every subsequent experience invited a nostalgic comparison, a comparison embellished by time. Whether it's the editorial page of *The New York Times,* or the network news, the American people are still unconsciously imbibing views distorted by that old romance. It was a constant theme of Cronkite, Smith, and Reasoner, and of Daniel's New York radio show *Insight.* Whenever the executive transgressed, these eastward-gazing pundits would refer in flattering terms to the British way, most often to Parliament's power to inhibit Executive trespass—an idea as distracting from reality as exquisite crocuses.

No wonder, then, that if alien commentators could respect such a deep tradition of hypocrisy, the native pundits should themselves be in confusion about the state of the nation:

> Britain is still the best country in the world for her citizens or her visitors. Democratic, tolerant, good-natured, skilled, resourceful and in some ways determined in her people, beautiful in her countryside and cultivated in her cities, Britain is still a nation to be envied.
>
> —THE LONDON *Times*

> British society is in a number of respects less cohesive than it was. Class divisions may be less conspicuous than in previous generations. Differences in income may matter less than they did, not because the position of the poor has been relatively improved but because with the general rise in prosperity more satisfactions are brought within everyone's grasp. But British society has become more atomized. There is a less clear sense of identity. The feeling of being part of a wider community is no longer so pronounced.
>
> —THE LONDON *Times,* A MONTH LATER

Some countries gain a sense of security from the will to change, the drive to improve. The British sense of security is precariously dependent on an opposite concept: the status quo. Keeping things as they are has an important motive: it keeps people where they are. Fear in one section of the community that their position is being eroded by another group is deeply founded: despite frequent gestures toward "leveling-up," most of the channels of privilege have survived. The upper classes resent the *nouveau riche;* the middle classes consolidate their own continuity; the working class has the satisfaction of somebody even less privileged to push around: the blacks. One group rides on the backs of the other. In a society where "progress" meant basically one class succeeding at the expense of another, "egalitarianism" has joined all the other myths to become, perhaps, the most dangerous of all. The longer it persists, the more divisive will be its final exposure. A series of tensions had been set up that run through British life. It is not so clearly drawn as the old class war—things have diffused into a cluster of separate conflicts involving class, ethics, morals, ideologies. The apparent coherence of Britain is an illusion, but an illusion that has been carefully engineered. None of it would hold together without a device the British invented: the gentleman's club.

Britain is run through an extensive network of private transactions. It is the most secretive ruling system in the Western world. The club, and variations of the club principle, are indispensable to these clandestine power networks. The visible and acknowledged clubs play a part in this process, but more important are the looser and more shadowy aggregations of vested interest and influence-peddling.

The principle of the club is the key to understanding how British society preserves its continuity. While the more flagrant superstructure of the class system apparently disappeared, it had merely gone underground.

The club is an underground circuit. If clubs hadn't already been invented, they would have had to come into being sooner or later. Today Britain is riddled with clubs. They range from the powerful to the powerless. At their most opaque they contain enormous influence.

The club is a cross between a tribal cell and a secret society. It is a game anybody can play: if you're an outsider to one club you can be an insider to the next. This game appeals to the British because it is a progressively elitist process. Clubs provide a perfect cover for discrimination. From the bottom to the top, each group becomes smaller until, at the top, it is at its most discriminating. And since election to a club requires the endorsement of those who are already in it, self-perpetuation by one class is guaranteed. The British form into clubs as fish form into shoals, as sheep into flocks, as Sicilians into families. But like the Mafia, the really important clubs have no formal shape, no overt structure. They are clusters of power in which the whole is larger than the parts but where the extent of the whole is impossible to measure. Of all these clusters, there are three that, between them, are decisive in the lives of the British. In descending order they are:

THE CUSTODIANS

In this supposedly model democracy, the country is not run by the people elected to run it. The power of Parliament has been systematically eroded, and real power lies elsewhere in the hands of the Custodians.

This elusive entity is more extensive than the old concept of "the Establishment." It outlives governments and fashions in politics. Not only is it unelected, it is self-recruiting and self-sustaining through the patronage of the club system.

The primacy of this kind of patronage underpins True Brit; True Brit created the Custodians and without it they would perish. It shapes their minds and it prescribes their actions. Behind every convulsion of this agonized country the conviction of the Custodians in this cause is absolute—they *are* the status quo. Change can come only on their terms, and to their advantage. The secret of their potency is continuity: twenty-five years of social flux have done nothing to disturb their tenancy. They are the wall on which every tide breaks and turns.

And yet the Custodians do not behave like an organized conspiracy. That would be too unsubtle. Following the laws of the club system, they have no formal mass. Their influence permeates the country from top to bottom, but it is never finite. Like amoebas they have no constant shape, and their intercourse is mysterious. They cluster, separate, and cluster again. The only clue to their habits is their fidelity to the traditional refuge of certain clubs.

The apparent epicenter of the Custodians' world is the clubs of Pall Mall and St. James's: the Athenaeum, The Travellers', the Carlton, Bucks, Brooks's, White's. These are still the switchboards through which many lines connect, and where many of their transactions take place. There are further identifiable outposts, like All Souls at Oxford, but the ancient colleges are no longer so convenient as they once were in days when politics and business were more leisured. In any case, all these older habitats of the elite were geared to less extensive and surreptitious dealing. Today the tracks of power disappear into the undergrowth, weaving to the discreetest outstation.

These privileged networks of the Custodians were a part of the social system that was supposed to collapse under the pressure of meritocracy and equality—themes which came late to the British, but which they acclaimed. This was, it is now clear, a cleverly intrigued deception. The Custodians have proved to be rather like one of those extraterrestrial invading armies in a science-fiction movie: every instrument of earthly resistance has been unleashed on them, the ground is thick with the clamor of battle, and then out of the smoke materializes the enemy—unscathed. What makes this feat more piquant is that it was a lucky accident. When the country turned from empire, it had to find a substitute role. The role it chose was sound enough: industrial and commercial expansion. Massive commitments were made. A civil service trained for and geared primarily to the climate of imperialism was redirected toward big business. But there were three ways in which this change diverged from the national character: socially, ethically, and technically. Socially, the profit motive was taboo. You could believe in it, pursue it, and prosper by it—but you didn't talk about it. It just wasn't done. This social convention led in turn to the ethical conflict. By its new standards, the country had to accept that the making of money, unalloyed hustling, should be an agreed motivation on the same plane that imperial conquest had once been. But to be as explicit as this ran against a strong cultural tradition: hustling was bad manners, bad breeding, and dubious ethically. The technical problem was equally one of habit: it concerned competence. Technical competence had never been highly valued or particularly expected. Consequently, it was in short supply.

There was no new body of competent men for the country to turn to for the management of its change of role. So the old one had to suffice. As it happened, this suited the Custodians perfectly. The loss of empire had once implied, for them, extensive redundancies. Now it was merely a question of changing hats, from ostrich plumes to bowlers. Their inaptness for the job was easily obscured. The process of business management was heavy in mystique. The Custodians exploited this by increasing the mystique to the point where they could claim to be the only ones who understood it, thereby resisting interference. If they could appropriate the right to run the corporate state, they would, in effect, be running the country. With some deft footwork, this is just what they did.

As Britain's power slides from second rank to third, the power of the Custodians is at its height. There is, perhaps, a fatal natural law in this, like the mating of the sockeye salmon—the journey upstream, against the odds, fulfilled in one great engulfing orgasm, then decay and death. True Brit provides that kind of obsessive quality.

THE LEAGUE OF GENTLEMEN

Bertrand Russell said that the "gentleman" was invented to symbolize the claims to power of a mixed class of aristocrats and industrialists. But the rank of gentleman has always been secondary; gentlemen are not the elite in Britain. The aristocracy still comfortably outranks them socially but has little influence in terms of real power. The Custodians' edge over the gentlemen is intellectual: they embody the idea of the "finest minds." This is the essence of their mystique. Social standing is crucial to the Custodians, but it is not enough. The gentleman, on the other hand, represents the triumph of manner over mind.

To join the League of Gentlemen, appearance matters more than substance. This appearance is not cheaply acquired; it is what many British public schools are in business to provide, at anything up to $2,500 a year basic charge. Nonetheless, there is a weakness in this arrangement. The components of the gentleman are wholly cosmetic, so that they lend themselves easily to counterfeit. The League of Gentlemen is full of fakes, the kind of men played in old British movies by Dennis Price and Richard Attenborough. The gentleman establishes his status merely by opening his mouth. In Britain a man is judged not so much by what he says as how he says it: accent and form of words, rather than content. Manner and style are everything, and without them money is dirt.

In the British corporate state a great deal was expected of the League of Gentlemen: they were supposed to provide the officer class of a new mercantile army. But it is now painfully clear that the qualities required of the gentleman are not those that make a modern business manager. The gentleman is self-centered, not corporately motivated or even noticeably loyal to the national interest. His prime concern is his own welfare. In order to follow this light, he has enjoyed a laxity of ethics unique in any business community.

A common myth about the gentleman is that he has scruples. As many who have had dealings with gentlemen will testify, they can be the most unscrupulous operators in the world. They are so plausible. There is their unwritten code—"the gentleman's agreement"; "the word of a gentleman is his bond." It has taken them far. But the cards are marked. It takes a gentleman to spot a gentleman—all others beware.

The gentleman is not much liked by the Custodians. To them business is a grubby trade; they are not, as will be amply evident, at their best in dealing with it. The gentleman finds his self-esteem not by looking up but by looking down. He discriminates against non-gentlemen with ruthless contempt. In London after World War I, society was so depleted by the carnage of the battlefield that, for a while, interlopers from below were allowed. They were called "temporary gentlemen." Once the bloodstock was replenished, out they went.

Gentlemen believe in True Brit. They should. It has provided their featherbed. They have been the factors of True Brit, trading on its bogus virtues in many a gullible marketplace. They do not like the new sales resistance to their tricks, a sign that style itself is no longer enough. Even at home there are rumblings of discontent. But one of the planks of the gentleman's ego is that he believes the world owes him a living. Just as it owes respect to the

British idea. He cannot grasp that his game is being called.

Under these pressures, the gentleman's ability to survive depends increasingly on the security of his club, the City of London, the largest financial and business center outside Wall Street. But even there the gentlemen have had to close their ranks. The defenses of the City have been breached. Men who come from no club, and who showed scant respect for the codes of the club system, have been successfully cashing in on the City's complacency. The Hustlers came to town, skillfully exploiting its soft spots and making unsettling waves. Harsh things have been said, and the barricades have been reinforced.

THE FIDDLERS

The Fiddlers are the outsiders who made their own inside. Excluded by both the Custodians and the League of Gentlemen, the Fiddlers could follow suit in one way: they got organized. From the Custodians they learned the value of clandestine power. They have taken their own slice of territory: local government. And from the League of Gentlemen they took an ethical lead: do anything, so long as you don't get caught.

The Fiddlers are the newest and most disconcerting of the clubs. Disconcerting, because they have shaken to its roots one of the last remaining myths of the British system—the picture of a selfless, industrious, and scrupulously honest grass-roots political fabric. In fact, the Fiddlers have come from that section of British society which was screwed by the League of Gentlemen for two hundred years. They spring from the clerical and trading classes, who served silently for so long while the fruits were picked by gentlemen. The Fiddlers had a ready-made social network, clubs with charitable intent like the Rotarians, or slightly wacky rituals, like the Freemasons. They also used to be God-fearing Anglicans, Baptists,

Congregationalists, Methodists. But suddenly they got the message that the man who preached on Sunday fiddled on Monday. As middle-class venality became more blatant, the outsiders wanted in. Their chance came almost by accident. All corrupt systems have to have a source of temptation. Until recently, temptation in large amounts was noticeably lacking from British local politics. The authorities had been starved of funds, the machine run on a shoestring. Then, in the early 1960s, huge sums were pumped into the coffers of the legislators to fund regional rebuilding programs. City politicians had a new power: architectural patronage. And they quickly learned the value of that patronage.

Contracts for new hospitals, schools, offices, city centers, and housing developments were the stuff that graft was made of. Much of the fiddling was small, operated within a cosy local fellowship in which politics, business, and social life overlapped with ease and discretion. Some of it escalated into wider, regional fellowships.

The more parochial the fiddling is, the better its protection. On that scale it fits snugly into familiar and matured circuits. The Fiddlers do not like people who get too big for their boots. Security lies in modesty. Fiddlers do not bother with True Brit—it is too blatant for their taste and they leave it to the gentlemen. True Brit touches their lives in only one way: the queen. Fiddlers are good monarchists.

4. THE CUSTODIANS

Men of Power, Feet of Clay

As Ian Fleming made the seedy British secret service seem sexy and omnipotent, the novels of Lord (C. P.) Snow have fantasized the British civil service as a race of intellectual supermen. There is a common trick: both make literary capital out of arcane skills, which allows greater scope for the imagination; secrecy surrounding the reality helps embellish the mythology. Take this passage from *Corridors of Power*, Snow's 1964 novel about Whitehall, in which he describes his quintessential senior civil servant, Hector Rose:

> They had given him the Grand Cross of the Bath, the sort of decoration he and his friends prized, but which no one

else noticed. He still worked with the precision of a computer.

Earlier, in *Homecomings,* Snow said of Rose that he had made himself "tougher-minded." The tough-minded administrator with the precision of a computer was as near to the performance of a senior Whitehall figure as James Bond's bedroom scoring rate is to a clerk in MI5. Snow is a power voyeur. To him the struggle for the mastery of the executive is almost libidinous. His fabrication of the super-civil servant has been widely accepted as life-sized. It is hardly an image that Whitehall would want to discourage. As a public relations exercise for the Custodians, it was timely and effective.

In the 1960s, the "tougher-minded" civil servants seemed to crop up all over, essential figures in the scenario of a "revitalized" Whitehall and the Gods of the British ideal. But Snow had, at least, been prescient in one thing. At the end of the 1950s, as the most vocal champion of the new technocracy, he went into combat with Professor F. R. Leavis in the debate of "the Two Cultures," Leavis standing for the arts and the old civilization. Snow defined his thesis in a famous series of Harvard lectures. Far more than he could realize, the tension between these two cultures became fundamental to the management of British policy. And it produced the paradox of the Custodians, steeped in the tradition of the arts, acquiring a massive extension of their influence through a science-based change of role. They had little to offer but their mythology, enlarged by Snow. With their talent incompatible with their purpose, catastrophe was inevitable.

A slightly unraveled, donnish man was talking, and reflecting on power and how it evaded him: "I knew there was this inner committee of permanent secretaries [heads of departments]. The basic economic strategy of the government was being planned by this collection of civil servants. How rarely could we ever have a discussion in the cabinet without it virtually having been made a *fait accompli* by the previous decisions behind the scenes."

The speaker was the late Richard Crossman who died in April, 1974, an ex-minister in the six-year Labour government of Harold Wilson, and a left-wing intellectual and party theoretician. He had been, he confessed, neutralized by the Custodians or—in his own words— "put into a Whitehall cocoon."

Crossman was not an exception. Wilson's own personal secretary, Marcia Williams, recalled afterward that her master, too, had been under the thumb and the spell of the civil service. He was, she said, "a civil servant *manqué*"—so bewitched by the mystique of the Custodians that they played on his awe and had their way.

The subversion of government by the Custodians is complete. It is their newest and most ominous achievement. It is the final extension of a system that ranges much wider than government and whose power is ancient. The remarkable thing is that it should have reached its ultimate strength just at the time when privilege and unchallenged power by continuity were supposed to be cast aside. When it comes to a choice between new or old power, the British have proved to be recidivists. All the key positions held by the Custodians have resisted more democratic recruitment. The judiciary, the ambassadors, the top brass of the army, navy, and Royal Air Force, and the heads of the major banks all come from the same social background as they did in 1939.

There are two tiers to the recruiting process of the British elite: the public schools and the universities of Oxford and Cambridge. The public schools are socially selective by both the level of their fees and the patronage of one class toward its own kind. Although the "Oxbridge" universities are in theory more competitive and less socially selective than they were, they have in reality done little or nothing to interrupt or dilute the traditional recruitment of the Custodians. Over 60 percent of English universities were created since 1950, and 50 percent since 1960—yet Oxbridge is unchallenged as the gate to power. Oxbridge is not only a source of higher education. It is the final filter for membership of the Custodians. It reflects in microcosm the values and mores that will govern the mature attitudes of those inducted into it. A strong psychological necessity is a feeling of superiority—not only social but vocational superiority. At Oxbridge the contacts with the scouting system of the Custodians are highly developed. The first taste a man gets of the informality of the process—a chance meeting here, a nod there, the development of a family connection, the social intercourse in which character is assessed in the most casual circumstances—show its style. To the right man, who will by dint of his earlier social conditioning find this a natural development and be at ease within it, the possibilities are great. To an undergraduate from a different social background, up from a state school or from a lesser public school and without both the connections and the social graces, the concept of equal opportunity begins to seem illusory.

This is the dividing line, for despite the lip service to equality of opportunity, the gaseous network of privilege has survived and adapted. Oxbridge sorts out the Custodians from the gentlemen. The inductees see that this is the way business should work, a fluid mating of ambition and opportunity, the "oral interview" in a country-house setting with the putative character being probed for the blemish of excess: too much zeal, too much lip, too much idealism. There must be the negative qualities, because it is axiomatic to the Custodians that they must preserve the British way by stopping things as much as by starting them. An elegant style in inertia is highly valued. It will be the benchmark of higher rank. As one ex-Whitehall executive puts it: "The average official would rather miss a dozen opportunities than make one mistake."

For all its discrimination, the selection filter of the Custodians can sometimes be disastrously indiscriminate. The unspoken and unwritten criteria depend implicitly on *laxity:* if a man passes muster by looking and sounding right, it is against the code to delve beyond the satisfactory veneer. If he looks wrong in the superficial things, if the diction is coarse at the edge, then his character will be pressed. If not, not.

This is the innate consent of clubmanship. Its most conspicuous disaster, one that left the process wounded but not overly repentant, was the case of the three spies Guy Burgess, Donald Maclean, and Kim Philby. They were all at Cambridge in the early 1930s, though not visibly linked. Burgess, loose, Bohemian, and homosexual, was nonetheless an old Etonian and had enough swagger to recover from dissipation and make it into British Intelligence by social manipulation and via *The Times* and the BBC. On the way he made an attempt to work for the Tory party's research department, abortive when the prospective employer complained, "But what about his *nails?*" Maclean, epicene but more personable, slipped easily into the diplomatic corps. Philby, the son of a diplomat who had managed both to belong to the Athenaeum and be a Muslim with two wives, was less flamboyant than his father and ingratiated himself so effectively into the ranks of the Custodians that he worked, at increasingly high levels, in the British Secret Service for three decades.

This trinity of dissemblers, plausible enough by background to get easily through the elitist filter, were all Soviet agents. When Burgess and Maclean defected to their masters, it ruptured relations between the British and the CIA. When Philby, the consummate double agent, capped his career with a passage to Moscow it left the Americans speechless. But that is not the end. There were two recruiting systems at work at Cambridge in the 1930s: the Custodians' and the Russians'. Whoever it was who saw through the veneer of these three into their treacherous hearts still, for all we know, sits in some corner of a London club among his fellows and muses on the certainty of his eye for talent. And if that was the most spectacular breach of the system, what other warps of mind and body have slipped through, malign or merely incompetent, to complete another shorted circuit? It is quite a thought.

It will be said that things don't work that way anymore. Then consider this. The middle and upper ranks of the Custodians are now the crop of the period between 1948 and 1960. And there is a salient bias in this generation that makes it unique. It contains by far the lowest proportion of graduates with mathematics or science degrees this century—just 4 percent. (The figure was 25 percent between 1905 and 1914 and had sunk to 12 percent by 1937.) This means that 96 percent of the leadership in Whitehall has the classic arts background of the civilized amateur. They are Greeks wrestling with the Roman world.

Correcting an error like this is like taking the wheel of a 200,000-ton oil tanker and trying to avoid a rock a few hundred yards ahead. It can't be done. A change made now would take until 1990 to work through.

This cultural bias is a serious form of corruption —benign, but disastrous in its consequences. What, according to the mythology of Snow, are often called "the top 2 or 3 percent of the country's brains" are the wrong kind of brains. The reason is that the social matrix is not the professional one; they don't match. The overwhelming preference for the arts over the sciences has bred the wrong elite. In Whitehall the priorities have switched from the proconsulate of empire in the Foreign Office to the domestic departments. The role of the civilized amateur survived in the colonies, but the demands of Britain without empire are different.

The power base of the Custodians splits into two sections—the roles of management and of control. The management roles are primarily domestic: in economic affairs, industrial policy, and the social departments, including health, welfare, and the services grouped under the jargon label of environment. The control roles are the traditional ones of the judiciary, the military, and the police. To the mind of the Custodian, the skills of business management are rude and grubby. He cannot grasp the redundancy of his training. In the jungle of industry he is credulous and yet arrogant, naïve and yet powerful. He cannot cope, he will not yield.

Unsuited by skill for the management role, the Custodians are now unsuited by temperament for the control role. While their contemporaries in Whitehall fumble from one catastrophe to another, the judiciary has become irascible with incomprehension. If society obligingly evolved at the same pace as the law, all would be well. But in Britain, as elsewhere, society is not so cooperative. And the British judiciary remains regally aloof from social upheaval. Among the senior judges (High Court and above), 79 percent in 1939 were products of Oxbridge, and more than 84 percent had the same background in 1971. The judges educated at public schools have stayed at a steady 80 percent. In Britain judicial insularity is either regarded as a harmless joke ("Tell me, pray, *what* are the Beatles?") or as a guarantee of objective detachment. The danger of falling out of touch with reality is unheeded.

Remoteness may once have been valued as a sign of position, in a society like Britain's built on deference. But a judiciary made to look ridiculous ceases to inspire awe.

The response of the Custodians has not been to recover their dignity by changing their ways but to try to sustain it by Draconian means.

Pigheadedness of this kind is inevitable in a self-perpetuating power structure, bent on its own preservation. It has been estimated that the sons of the British elite are five times more likely to inherit that position than a boy in the middle class is likely to attain it. For a working-class child to end up at the top the odds are still 50 to 1 against. The value of this tradition is not lost on the odd *arriviste* who breaks through. Lord Snow, a meritocrat of modest background, put his own son into Eton and explained, "It seems to me that if you are living in a fairly prosperous home, it is a mistake to educate your child differently from most of the people he knows socially." Eton and Winchester still offer such an inside track to power that one researcher has called them "conspiracies rather than eduational establishments."

For more than a decade, through an incremental process they did not initiate, the running of the country has passed into the hands of the Custodians. It cannot easily be won back. Their power is drawn from a social and class system that seems inviolate. Nothing could be more incongruous.

Her hair is gray now, but the eyes are clear and wise. She, too, has pulled back from the fight, though from the other side. Dame Evelyn Sharp was Richard Crossman's Custodian, reaching an Olympian height for a woman civil servant. But her experience of power has given her pause. After she retired, she told a BBC interviewer, "Changes in the organization and machinery of our system of government are overdue: some are being made, but not, to my way of thinking, enough, and they are nothing like radical enough. We're much too complacent about our parliamentary and ministerial system. The real peril is that we may suddenly become frightened by the way things appear to be going and in our fright look for a more authoritarian form of government—*and there are people waiting in the wings.*"

"The Establishment" in its old sense provided a means of identifying a power collective that was amorphous. It did have certain formal routes through which it worked: the courts, the executive, the institutions. Acting singly and openly through any one of these bases, the established powers could be detected. The value of the term "Establishment" was as shorthand, to explain covert action by some mysterious will. Thus a scapegoat like Stephen Ward in the Profumo affair could be described, correctly, as the victim of a "vengeful Establishment" when there was no clearer explanation and when the actual conspirators could not be named. The regressive instinct of a ruling elite could be sensed rather than seen.

There will always be these dark currents of mood running behind the exercise of power in Britain. They can sometimes build up in strength against a change in the tolerances of society until they surge against it in the open. A rare instance of this kind of pressure becoming explicit, rather than showing itself through a series of unexplained repressions, arose from that sexual *cause célèbre,* the trial for obscenity of the underground magazine *Oz.*

Although he moderated the original sentences on appeal, the lord chief justice warned, "We would like to make it quite clear in general terms that any idea that an offense under the Obscene Publications Act, 1959, does not merit a prison sentence should be eradicated. *There will be many cases in future in which a prison sentence is appropriate. . . .*"

The bench does not often reveal its sentiments or its intentions like this, or even suggest the prejudgment of future cases.

As convenient as it is, the use of the label "the Establishment" to describe any collective act by covert groups is now obsolete. It gained currency when the traditional institutions were still relatively undisturbed by modern pressures. Since then there has been an extensive redistribution of power in Britain. This has been achieved at the expense of principles and elements that were thought basic to that mystical entity, the British Constitution. It has made power harder to identify. It has created new groupings, coalitions, alliances, and concentrations of interests and power outside the experience or understanding of most of the country. Although these forces are novel, the temper of the power collective is still strongly conservative, even reactionary. It has at heart the most hardening of self-interests, the conservation of wealth and privilege. There are no countervailing forces.

"The Establishment" will no longer do as a label, because it minimizes the problem. To the older vested social and financial interests has been added a rapacious new one, an Orwellian bureaucratic machine that more and more seems to transcend simple human drives like cupidity and ambition. Its motivation is the preservation, at all costs, of the British way.

5. RITUAL AS THE MARK OF IMPOTENCE

Parliament Drowns in Words, the Monarchy Hangs in There

When a British institution ceases to work, it is not discarded: function fades into ritual, reality is overtaken by myth. This kind of metamorphosis is exemplified by the monarchy. What few people have yet grasped is that Parliament, that eternal torch of the Anglophile, has followed the monarchy into illustrious impotence. It is the symbol of democratic consultation long after it has ceased to exercise any real power.

A curious by-product of the ritualizing process is that, once embalmed in this way, an institution earns more reverence and respect than it enjoyed when effective. Politicians themselves have fallen lower and lower in esteem, but Parliament as an abstraction is more loved —not for what it is but for what it represents. It is as though the mock-Gothic shell of the Palace of Westminster, disembodied from its occupants, has become a temple to which prayers are offered in the hope of national redemption.

It is the Custodians who have made a eunuch of Parliament, but it is a case of castration by consent. The defenders of Parliament recognized the threat, but they have been rendered harmless by their own romanticism, one of the move naïve British delusions. The struggle has produced some strange bedfellows. None are more apparently incompatible than Michael Foot, a doctrinaire and brilliant left-winger, and J. Enoch Powell, the right wing's most cherished politician. Foot says, "I believe that powerful forces and powerful people are engaged in trying to destroy the House of Commons." The only fault in this statement is that it predicts something that has already taken place. But what is his remedy? The same as Powell's, which is: "Everything which diminishes true debate on the floor of the House of Commons strengthens the executive and weakens Parliament." Both of them regard rhetoric as a form of magnetic field that, once created, automatically repels usurpers. But the irony is that Parliament has died in the spell of its own voice.

The procedures and powers of Parliament ossified over the last hundred years. During the same period the role of the Custodians moved gradually from a clerical to a managerial one. Parliament was so busy talking to itself that it failed to see the inference of this trend and its own vulnerability to it. A love of language has never been more fatal. Those who succumbed to it believe that debate is one of the British acts of genius, and that words gracefully mustered and elegantly deployed have the power of an army, rather than that they are a substitute for action or knowledge. Listen, for example, to Brian Walden, a Labour M.P. When it was suggested that Parliament should counter the transgressions of the Custodians with expert inquisitorial committees, like Senate committees, he said this was the kind of notion put forward by people who "see politics as a science and prefer it that way. They don't want it as an art."

This was another echo of Lord Snow's clash of the cultures, the Greeks versus the Romans. "Art" is no answer to Parliament's collapse. The House of Commons, whatever its grander illusions, has several rather basic purposes. It is supposed to make the laws, police the executive, and represent the public's concern for the way its money is spent. Government expenditure now runs at $40 billion a year and is expected to double within a decade. The disposal of these funds gets only the most perfunctory supervision from Parliament, which is kept in a state of consenting ignorance.

The notion beloved of the Anglophiles among American newscasters of Parliament as a snarling watchdog is risible when subjected to examination. For much of the time in the House of Commons only a handful of M.P.'s are present, even for important legislation. A full house can be provoked only by a theatrical sense of crisis. Normally, while one or other of the parties has its spokesman droning on, other members are slumped on the benches in some idle trance. One or two will be sound asleep. Others will be dozing in the library or drinking in the smoking room. The most animated places are the bars, where the village gossip of Westminster transcends weightier issues. Many M.P.'s won't be anywhere near the place. If they are Tories, they will be attending to various business interests; if they are Labour, they will be God knows where.

Parliament's faith in the powers of oratory puts more dependence on symbols than on actual institutional power. Powell talks of recovering "the sheer pride in being a member of this sovereign assembly." The word *sovereign* is a key to the emotional defenses of the British idea, standing for something that is threatened not only from within but by nasty European and alien habits. Sov-

ereignty is like virginity—you're never the same without
it. Say "sovereignty" to John Bull and he growls with vigilant loyalty. It is all a charade, and it simply makes life
easier for the real enemies of Parliament by diverting attention from them. And there is no doubt about their tactics.

In extending their province, the Custodians have
drowned Parliament in paper. In 1938, 935 pages were
put on the Statute Book by Parliament. By 1971 it was
2,100 pages. Sir William Armstrong, who as head of the
civil servants under the Home office feeds legislation into
Parliament, admits, "The mass is so great that an awful
lot of it is going to get overlooked by the sheer size of it."
George Cunningham, a former civil servant who is now
an M.P., sets out the name of the game more clearly:
"The government is in theory subject to the approval of
Parliament. In practice it has no scrutiny from Parliament
at all. The legislature is not only totally uninfluential but
doesn't even try to influence the specific purposes for
which money is voted."

Secrecy about money is obsessive. One government
after another has refused to disclose its medium-term expenditure plans, the allocations that really show a government's priorities. Without seeing such a basic tool of
money management, Parliament has negligible influence
on policy. This concealment is defended on remarkably
specious grounds. One minister, Patrick Jenkin, said that
if the government revealed how much it thought incomes
would rise, the labor unions would immediately submit
claims for wage increases based on the estimates. And,
giving away the real motive, he added, "Parliament cannot become in any sense responsible for policy."

This is really the voice of the Custodians, with the
minister playing the ventriloquist's dummy. Public expenditure is the root of real power in the corporate state: if
Parliament has no control over that—and it hasn't—the
substance of its role is gone.

The Custodians spend public money like drunken sailors, but their binges are revealed only after the event. Parliament's main whistle-blowing body is the Public Accounts Committee. An auditor general with six hundred accountants serves this committee, but its reports become inquests, not deterrents. To its questions the Custodians provide pathetic and evasive answers. Essential information can be withheld on the most spurious pretexts. In ten years no detailed information on either expenditure or performance was given to the committee about the Concorde SST, on the grounds of "commercial confidentiality."

The preference for hindsight (a word frequently used by the Custodians hauled in front of the Public Accounts Committee) over foresight is devastatingly clear from the disposition of teeth to the "watchdogs." Against the PAC's six hundred accountants, the body supposed to audit spending as it happens, the Select Committee on Expenditure, has a staff of barely a dozen. Everything is organized to give the profligate executive the least amount of trouble.

But the furtive administrators can occasionally be jerked out of their leisurely rhythms. When Parliament insists on a piece of legislation being swiftly implemented, against the preference of the executive, the Custodians have to yield. But there is a catch. They regard this as "rushing through," a relative term in Whitehall. Under this kind of pressure things get mysteriously screwed up. Sir William Armstrong unguardedly reveals the ploy: "Frequently acts of Parliament are passed, then after a little while an amending act is brought in, the thing is adapted and adjusted, and it seems fairly clear, looking back on it, that perhaps the first one was brought in a little faster than it need have been."

In other words, play it our way or else.

"Adapting" and "adjusting," two seemingly innocent terms full of manipulative promise, are supposed to be the functions of the parliamentary committees that consider legislation as it is transmuted from a bill to an act. These committees are contrived to give the appearance of bipartisan consultation. In reality it is an empty, time-wasting gesture. The government does whatever it sets out to do, under the impress of the Custodians. For example, in one period when 865 amendments were proposed by ministers to their own legislation, 864 were passed. Of 688 amendments asked for by M.P.'s not in the government, 39 were passed. M.P.'s are ostensibly chosen for these committees on the grounds of appropriate expertise. But their ideas fall on deaf ears if they conflict with the preordained wishes of the executive. In at least one case it was literally deaf ears: during the four and a half months' passage of one bill, a government supporter on the committee wore earplugs throughout.

If dissenting M.P.'s can make no impression, more clandestine pressures can. As the line between government and business dissolves, lobbying by vested interests using their captive M.P.'s, and by more covert ministerial routes, is applied with effect. This is the major reason why both the Labour and Conservative parties were reluctant to accept a register open to public scrutiny of all financial and business connections of M.P.'s. Many members, particularly Tories, are so embroiled in business that Parliament is little more to them than a moonlighting exercise with expedient uses.

The kind of thing that *is* taken seriously in Westminster is the trivia of etiquette. As in this exchange:

MR. WILSON: What Mr. Heath is saying about the Labour Party is a lie. (*Loud Conservative protests and Labour cheers.*)
MR. HEATH: If Mr. Wilson uses unparliamentary language that is a matter for him. (*Loud interruptions.*)

When, after deliberation, the Speaker of the House deprecated the use of the word "lie," Wilson withdrew it and substituted "a pack of lies." After further deliberations the Speaker ruled that "a pack of lies" was also contrary to the established etiquette and should not be used again. Also banned are "that is a lie," "he is lying," "liar," "deceiving," "deliberately misleading," and "a damn lie" —together with "dog," "cheeky young pup," "guttersnipe," "rat," "stool pigeon," and "swine."

In earlier days Parliament was more robust and, probably, more honest. It was certainly more effective. The blanding of language shows the graying and more euphemistic preferences of an institution that, like the courts, resorts to dignity as a substitute for virility. Parliament is more and more locked out of its own time by ritual. As one unusually realistic Tory puts it: "Our procedure over the last hundred years or more has been very largely unchanged. Before we preach to Europe about how it should organize its affairs, we have a special duty to put our own house in order."

The daily "grilling" of ministers in the House of Commons is a masquerade. The conditions under which questions are put are carefully controlled. Sometimes this amounts to rigging. The accepted convention is that questions can be planted to enable a minister to say something in a reply that he cannot present as an unprovoked statement—a partisan piece of boasting, for example. This pretense came unstuck in a case where a Conservative minister fed two dozen "questions" to tame supporters to block an attack by the Opposition. The dummy questions were drafted by civil servants, not even the minister. When these dirty tricks were revealed in the *Sunday Times,* the official response was a pious statement about "impropriety."

Another sham procedure is the "lobby" system. This requires journalists to cover events that never happen. Reporters accredited to the Westminster lobby agree to attend briefings on the basis that they are "nonattributable" and "off the record." Such briefings are often used by politicians for kite-flying to test public opinion on a policy. British journalists are content with the servility of this function; they believe that they need the politicians more than the politicians need them, an idea that would be novel in Washington. These tame dogs take their scraps at feeding time and wag their tails gratefully— unless something goes wrong. One Conservative minister who planted a story by this means saw it faithfully splashed over the front pages of several papers. But the "leak" misfired (it had misstated government policy). The minister was nevertheless able to sit silently by as Edward Heath denied that any briefing had taken place. The dogs yelped, but they soon subsided into compliance.

All the lesser deceits amplify the major one—that what happens in the House of Commons has real meaning. The mother of Parliaments is in her dotage, complacent and impotent. Ironically, Parliament seen purely as an abstraction is, like the monarchy, rated high in the public esteem while the M.P.'s themselves have slipped badly. One poll has placed M.P.'s eighth on an index of trustworthiness—doctors, judges, lawyers, civil servants, cabinet ministers, union leaders, and even local legislators are rated higher than M.P.'s, in that order. The M.P.'s have one consolation. The only people whose integrity is as suspect as their own are journalists.

In the end, though, it is not the public cynicism toward M.P.'s that has undermined Parliament but the self-absorption of the politicians and their own gullibility. The intoxicating ambience of Westminster, its introversion, and the kind of spiritual faith that is thought to secure the unwritten British Constitution have created Parliament's powerlessness. With Britain's entry into Europe the romanticism has, if anything, intensified. The phobias aroused by bureaucrats in Brussels are more impelling than the deep subversion of power at their doorstep.

Parliament is the latest British institution to complete the transition from a working instrument to a ritualistic myth; the first to do so was the monarchy. But where Parliament is pointless without its power, the monarchy has, with its impotence, gained a role.

The monarchy's importance as an institution rests on its placebo effect. It works because it has no power. It has no power because it is above power. If the ultimate allegiance of the people were to anything less mythical— to a general, a politician, even (like the French) to a banker—the current morbidity would make the head of state very insecure. Disenchanted generals in Britain cannot enforce their views with a coup d'etat because it is not the prime minister they would have to depose, but the crown. That is unthinkable. (The crown would also be proof against cabals of businessmen.)

Even when a political decision divides the country on issues of patriotism, as it did with the unilateral declaration of independence by the white supremacists of Southern Rhodesia, the queen manages to appear neutral, and it is impossible to guess where her sympathies lie. The Rhodesians still swear allegiance to the throne, believing themselves to be more British than the British. At the same time they are stigmatized as rebels against the crown. No contradiction seems apparent. In the same way, the erosion of "sovereignty" required by Britain's joining the Common Market needed the formality of royal assent, and nobody thought to ask whether the queen actually liked being diminished in this way.

The fiction that the queen plays an assenting and advising role in government is religiously sustained by politicians. At their weekly audience with the queen, prime ministers are now allowed to sit, rather than stand. This concession literally swept Harold Macmillan off his feet. Asserting that the influence of the monarch has actually increased, he recalls:

> The Queen has a right as well as a duty to be fully informed of all the affairs not only of the United Kingdom

but also of all the countries of the Commonwealth, as well as of foreign countries. This duty was always conscientiously performed. All Cabinet papers, all departmental papers, all foreign telegrams are sent to her, and carefully studied by her. All the Cabinet's decisions which, under the Cabinet Secretarial system, are rapidly and accurately circulated, are available to her immediately . . . the Queen has the absolute right to know, to criticise, to advise.

This picture of royal dedication to the affairs of state is hard to swallow. All cabinet ministers complain that they can't get through their own papers. The prospect of digesting every day this cataract of words would be daunting even for somebody with nothing else to do, and nobody imagines that the queen is that dedicated. Macmillan's account is sycophantic drivel. The most assiduously studied paper in Buckingham Palace is *Sporting Life,* for its extensive coverage of horse racing. Nothing moves the royal adrenaline like the scent of the turf.

The monarchy isn't in need of propping up or being made to look industrious by politicians. It is the necessary fantasy. It was a happy accident that gave the country a queen when it did. A king would not have been right; the mood would not have favored him. A patriarch without an empire would have been too clearly redundant, too much the last of the Romanovs, too much a reminder of what had passed.

But a queen, especially one capable of turning from a fairy princess into a homely matron, offers succor to the depleted ego. As the country turns in on itself, it needs her maternal embrace. There is no other bosom to cry upon, and certainly none more commodious. This is not the brave "second Elizabethan Age" proclaimed at her coronation, but a maudlin time that this dull and safe woman suits well. As long as she remains, the crown will seem relevant. When she goes, it may not be as secure.

The court of Elizabeth II is a shrewdly stage-managed fantasy, part De Mille, part Ruritanian, part

Noël Coward, part P. G. Wodehouse (who else was the Duke of Windsor but Bertie Wooster?). Over the years the monarchy has learned to adapt, though often more in appearance than in fact. The royal family has been deformalized but not demystified—it is a delicate change. Its duties have been made to look onerous, while its comforts have remained lavish. It has kept its riches but successfully pleaded penury. It has appeared united, the exemplary nuclear family, while riven with temperaments.

When the queen asked Parliament for more money, there were hysterical attempts to justify it. Her advisers produced a list of her arduous duties. She could never take "a complete holiday" (she spends a third of every year in her rural castles). Even her acknowledged recreations are portrayed as dutiful: "The queen and the royal family are well known as supporters of sport and athletics." The domestic touch is not neglected: "As well as carrying the exceptional burdens of sovereignty, the queen carries also those duties common to all wives and mothers." And, leaving nothing to chance: "The queen is an owner-breeder of thoroughbred racehorses, and her successes on the turf give pleasure to a large section of the public who are interested in breeding and racing."

Since the queen's accession, the cost of running the show has gone from $3 million to $11.7 million a year, a rise of 280 percent. While the queen herself needn't have resorted to a contrived defense of her way of life, the comforts of her relatives are a more vulnerable point. Her mother's household includes two peers, seven army officers, a mistress of the robes, two ladies of the bedchamber, three extra ladies of the bedchamber, four women of the bedchamber, and six extra women of the bedchamber. The bedchamber must be action central.

The queen's sister, Princess Margaret, is probably the least popular of the whole family. She has been called "this expensive kept woman" by one M.P. Her house has cost the taxpayer $200,000 so far, and she gets $87,500 a year, tax free. But it is not so much these expenses that displease the public as her glowering demeanor and increasingly dowdy appearance. As one sister has become mature and steady as the monarch, the other seems to have gone sour and irascible. Something of the same mood afflicts Lord Snowdon. Life in the glass cage has not worked out too well for him.

But the most volatile temperament in the royal family is Prince Philip's. For a man who was penniless when he married into the family and who now gets $163,000 a year from the public coffers, as well as a hefty subsidy from his wife, Philip seems singularly impatient with his patrons. He leads the life of a royal James Bond, switching from helicopter to private plane to racing yacht to fast car to royal yacht as he swings annually around the world, usually managing to be in agreeable corners of the South Pacific and other temperate zones when the British winter is at its worst. In 1971, for example, he was able on his own to visit, among other places, Grand Bahama, the Galapagos Islands, Fiji, New Guinea, Australia, Bahrain, and Iran. The royal yacht, *Britannia*, on which his three-month winter cruise took place, costs $2.5 million a year to run.

All this activity is presented as a selfless endurance test carried out in the public interest. Lord Cobbold, the lord chamberlain, is so anxious to uphold the idea that Philip has sacrificed all for the crown that he has actually said, "It seems only reasonable to me that in the case of someone doing a full-time job and precluded from earning the high salary which he would undoubtedly command in the outside world, there should be a considerable element of real remuneration." The only "outside job" that could match Philip's income and life-style is held down by Aristotle Onassis, and the two do, at least, have a bond of Greek birth.

In the early 1940s George VI and his queen had "arranged" the courtship of their daughter Elizabeth and

Prince Philip Mountbatten. Snobs in London society dis-
approved. They thought the couple were too interre-
lated. The Mountbattens' most Anglicized representative
was the young Elizabeth's cousin, Lord Louis. The blood
of Prince Philip Mountbatten mingled the royal lines of
Denmark, Germany, and Greece, but the Continental
monarchies were crumbling. Philip's father, Prince Andrew, was content to play out the role of the philandering
Ruritanian on the Riviera, while Philip was being
"blooded" in battle with the Royal Navy, under the tute-
lage of Lord Louis. The Battle of the Mediterranean, tough
as it turned out to be, must have been preferable to an aim-
less life among the discards of the old thrones (although
Philip's professional dedication to the navy went with a
touch of his father's roving eye). His emergence in Westminster Abbey in 1947 as the handsome fairy prince
slowed him down a bit, but the frequent cracking of his
cool since then is an obvious sign of chafing at the bit.

All the same, the British public is very forgiving.
Philip makes sober matrons swoon, and even Labour
prime ministers have been known to genuflect. He
shrewdly knows how much rope is available to him, and he
uses all of it. The principal victims of his public outbursts
are well chosen: journalists. It is a target that the British
would choose themselves. So that when, as he has, Philip
throws nuts at both the Barbary apes and reporters in Gibraltar, or tells photographers in Jamaica that they are
"bloody clots," or says to another photographer in Beirut
"Stuff that camera up your ass," he is sure that these
trained masochists will both report his actions and turn
the other cheek. There is something feisty in the prince
that the British would like to see in other public figures
—the boorish Aryan who can keep the natives down.

His actual contribution is negligible. He sponsors
Teutonic-style expeditions for young men who fancy the
rugged life; he promotes the preservation of wildlife
while his daughter rides with impunity with the foxhunt-

ers; he gives occasional jingoistic speeches exhorting exporters to bigger deals; he endorsed the diplomatic relationship with Fascist states like Portugal. There is not really a job there, but his public relations are, usually by his own devising, expertly managed. And that is, after all, what keeps the fantasy of monarchy viable.

Philip's short fuse has been inherited most noticeably by his daughter. The constraints on the life of a young princess are not what they were when Princess Margaret was sternly discouraged by the Archbishop of Canterbury from marrying Peter Townsend, the rakish Battle of Britain hero. But for a girl with the drives of Anne they are still enough to provoke frequent minor rebellions. She once cut a swath through the socially approved but effete young stags of London. As well as being headstrong like her father, Anne has contracted her mother's horse mania. The listless and decorative life that might otherwise have been her lot has been replaced by dedication to the saddle. This, in turn, diverted her from the playgrounds of the *Almanac de Gotha* into the arms of the British squirearchy, a close-knit society where the horse is god.

It is also the breeding ground of another kind of thoroughbred, the kind of young man who once went off with the Hussars to the Peninsular War. He is a fusion of sportsman and soldier. It is not a world where brains count for much. Physical courage is at a premium. When Anne met her dragoon it was soon clear who was the stronger of the two personalities. Mark Phillips was awed by Anne as both horsewoman and companion. As a husband he is helped by the esoteric bond of the equestrians; both he and Anne could ride horses before they could walk. But he's going to find his wife as hot-blooded as any young filly. She is extremely competitive and strong-willed, and the marriage is going to be more public and more eventful than any in the royal family since Wallis Simpson found her king.

The wedding of Anne and Mark Phillips obliged the national psychology. Another pageant in Westminster Abbey, an orgy of ritualistic sentiment, was the kind of tonic Britain sorely needed. In this sense the royal family is an impeccably trained branch of show business. They know just how to open the withering glands of national pride, to conjure the last juices from the most cynical breast. It is the one thing they do really well, and for which there is no substitute. Coming at a time of increasing disenchantment with the Common Market, and during a state of emergency, the wedding seemed also to be an aggressive reassertion of all the mythical Anglo-Saxon qualities, an answer to the bland and anonymous sovereignty of the bureaucrat.

But it was really too late. Brussels is already closer than Westminster Abbey. The old monarchs might spin in their tombs, but the run is nearly over.

Perhaps Prince Charles senses his own impending redundancy. By the time he becomes king the country will be unrecognizable. His subjects will be governed by European laws. His Parliament, already enfeebled, will be no better than a rubber stamp. His country will be paved over and cemented to Europe by the umbilical needs of the corporate state, like a none-too efficient manufacturing subsidiary. With these imperatives, the monarchy will lose credence. Minds that care little for palaces and castles are going to be increasingly impatient to find them still occupied. The royal family will become the reproving ghosts of a lost identity.

For the moment, the queen puts a stoic face on things. She is not shrewish, she is not imperious (once the only persona for a monarch), she is not neglectful, and she is not in any way ridiculous. She seems to want to be accepted as more real, but how real can a queen be? She has been trying public-relations tricks like "walkabouts," to suggest a more touchable monarch. But these produce brief and often awkward chats with the plebs and change nothing. The queen obviously wishes that they were convincing, but the glass cage filters out too much reality. It is unnatural for her to be natural.

The English millennium was reached in 1973. In 973 King Edgar was crowned at Bath, becoming by legend the first King of England. But it depended on what was meant by England. There was another claimant, Egbert, crowned King of England in 829, which—if valid—made the millennium more than 130 years late. Nonetheless, Elizabeth II, the matronly housefrau of German lineage, was happy to endorse Edgar's claims because it seemed a good time to boost the British idea with a piece of pageant.

In its present state the monarchy is relatively harmless—relative, that is, to the corrupting and corrupted political monarchies of the American and French presidencies. The queen is at least above all that, and although she stays above it by being in the clouds, it is not bad for people to be able to look up occasionally. Especially if it takes their eyes and minds off the mess below.

The euphoric effect of the monarchy is not lost on the British press. A royal wedding can wipe all news, especially bad news, off not only the front page but virtually every page. Twenty-four hours after the nation had stopped to watch Anne take her Mark, the London *Times* could still accord this event more space than the worst economic emergency since the war. The complicity of the press in sustaining Britain's Pollyanna tendency is manifest.

A country that is constantly taken by surprise as it falls apart is being kept in the dark by the people who are supposed to be shining the light. Surprise is, after all, the child of ignorance. The British don't know why things are so bad for them because they aren't being told. One reason why they're not being told is that the press is dilatory. Another reason is that the architects of the disaster enjoy the most effective security blanket in any supposedly democratic system.

Richard Crossman, a former Leader of the House of Commons and a constitutionalist, said that British government is "the biggest coverer-up that's ever been." He recalled that nearly twenty years after the Suez imbroglio many of the details of the collusion between British and French governments are still safely locked away. There was a massive deception of Parliament, but no inquiry.

In a society like America, bruised into cynicism by successive scandals in the highest places, it is still possible to find the system redeeming because of the visibility of its corruption and the tradition of exposing it. Britain prefers the pretense that the privacy of power is essential to maintain its integrity, a reversion of logic that is defended assiduously. The parliamentary system assumes that accountability rests with ministers because they hold the power. Discounting the sham of parliamentary procedure from this assumption, it would still be meaningless, because the real power that needs to be held accountable is not there anyway.

It is no coincidence that the most oppressive part of institutionalized secrecy in Britain dates from the inchoate phase of the central bureaucracy. In the course of one sleepy afternoon in the late summer of 1911, the House of Commons passed the Official Secrets Act with only the most casual scrutiny and debate. It was an astute piece of timing by the executive. There was a widespread paranoia about German spies, and the new legislation seemed to be an essential strengthening of national security. But this was deceptive. Although the first section of the act was indeed aimed at espionage, the second part gave the bureaucrats an unprecedented degree of confidentiality, at the time when their power to intervene in the life of the country was to steadily escalate.

The combining of the two motives in one act judged

the British mood expertly. An act giving civil servants immunity to inconvenient surveillance would, on its own, have been too conspicuous. But put alongside the preservation of national security in the face of the dreadful Huns, it became tangled in patriotism. The impression was easily created that to challenge the Official Secrets Act was against the national interest—more than insolence, it was treachery. This deception held good for more than sixty years. Under its cover the Custodians have not only consolidated their hold, they have assumed a perpetual right to subversive activity.

Some of the things that the British are not allowed to know about those who rule them show how great is the arrogant self-assurance allowed by tradition. They also show the difference between apparent and real power. At the center of government the decision-making rests not so much with ministers as with sixteen cabinet committees. Neither the names nor the composition of these committees are disclosed. The Cabinet Office's explanation is:

> The decisions of these committees, as indeed the decisions of individual Ministers, are as much decisions of the Government as are decisions of the Cabinet itself. No Government, therefore, discloses the list of their committees, their membership or scope, for to do so would be liable to impair collective responsibility as well as detract from the individual responsibility of Ministers.

A more explicit denial of the principle of accountability could hardly be imagined. In effect this is saying that neither collective nor individual decisions can be traceable. From this it follows that policies and decisions should be seen as completely impersonal, conceived in a vacuum. Business executives would find this idea congenial. On these principles there is no way for either Parliament or the public to know on what grounds a crucial decision has been taken, or of understanding its motivation or judging its quality. The results are not exactly reassuring. For example, one of the secret committees is the Regional Policy and Environmental Committee, controlling projects involving about $50 billion of public money. It is the clearinghouse for airports, expressways, and edifices of all kinds.

It is in work of this kind that secrecy takes on the justification of "expertise." Planners develop a kind of "project maternalism"; their babies are so long in gestation that any challenge to their conception provokes an intense and jealous protectiveness. Their objective is to conceal their real intentions until the projects are beyond recall. And they do it with impunity. A leak of plans to curtail the national railroad network was enough to send Scotland Yard's Special Branch interrogating reporters and editors, searching their files and hounding them at their homes. This was the mechanism of the police state in action, carried out under the pretext of the Official Secrets Act.

But the act was challenged, and it did seem possible that it had fatally overreached itself. The *Sunday Telegraph* published a confidential British military report on Nigeria. Compared to the Pentagon Papers, it was a trifle, but in Westminster the government's reaction was apoplectic. After a controversial trial, Mr. Justice Caulfield threw out the government's case and said the Official Secrets Act should be "pensioned off." Some time later he explained that what really worried him was the way the act could be "viciously or capriciously used by an embarrassed executive." When a liberal judge talks like this, suspicion of the executive can't be lightly dismissed as radical paranoia.

Certainly the Custodians are agile in dealing with threats to their security. They proposed an Information Act to replace the Secrets Act. The use of a positive word like *Information* ought to have been a warning; language was being manipulated. This new device was outlined to the House of Commons under circumstances strangely similar to the somnolent debate of 1911 and showed perfectly the negligence of Parliament. It was a Friday in summer and many M.P.'s had already left town; the chamber was sparsely attended. At first the new act was taken at face value, as a reform. Then it became clear, when the official ambiguities were deciphered, that the real purpose was to put an even tighter clamp on government. The pivotal cabinet committees would remain invisible, and all decision-making would stay anonymous. There was no intention of following the lead of the American Freedom of Information Act, which critics had called for. In America the onus is on the government to justify a refusal to disclose material; in Britain any civil servant disclosing information faces criminal charges (in Sweden he faces charges if he does not). But the British system goes well beyond the concealment of contemporary decision-making. All government papers are kept from public scrutiny for thirty years; some, defined as "highly sensitive," are official secrets for one hundred years.

By parliamentary convention, a government can make any subject taboo simply by persistently refusing to answer questions about it. The list of such subjects now includes affairs as grave as "the day-to-day matters" of the White Fish Authority, forecasts of changes in food prices, the trade statistics for Scotland, discipline in schools, and the operation of ferry services. More significantly, it also includes details of arms sales (Britain is a major clandestine gunrunner), accident rates of aircraft, telephone taps, the reasons for allowing a merger, and details of sterling balances. The priorities between the public interest and private government are clear.

Where, in the face of all this suppression, are the scavengers of the press?

British newspapers include some of the most salacious and trivial in the world. Like the country itself, the newspapers adhere to class allegiances. You are what you

read. At the top you read *The Times* or, if you claim a
social conscience, *The Guardian.* The bourgeoisie read the
Daily Telegraph which, like its readers, practices the native
hypocrisies by concealing under a gray exterior an alert
eye for fruity courtroom details. The plebs take either the
Daily Mirror, now getting a little hard in the arteries, or
The Sun, the impudent and appalling creation of an
Australian interloper, Rupert Murdoch. Drifting in the
middle, with the confusions of the lower middle class, are
the *Daily Mail* and the *Daily Express.* The *Express* is the
most blatantly racist paper in Britain and stands to the
last with the white supremacists of Rhodesia. The only
consistently aggressive and serious journalism comes on
Sunday, in *The Observer,* the *Sunday Times,* and, occasionally, the *Sunday Telegraph.* To balance this, Sunday
also produces the *News of the World,* known to its 16 million readers as the "Screws of the World." Its view of the
world is exclusively carnal; this was the paper that performed the public service of photographing—but not
printing the resulting photographs of—Lord Lambton
with his pants down. It was also the paper that exposed a
sex payola system at the BBC. Rupert Murdoch, who
owns the *News of the World,* too, has shown a fine instinct
for winning readers and losing influence.

The combined artillery of the press (to use Jeffer-
son's phrase) produces not so much a bang as a whimper.
It is no match for the clandestine government. Where
vigilance matters most, British editors are blind. Their reporters are still where the power is supposed to be, in
Westminster, rather than where it is, in Whitehall, which
is only a couple of blocks away but could be a thousand
miles. Not one London paper has a reporter assigned to
Whitehall. The understanding of central government gets
scant regard.

The lapdogs of the Westminster lobby don't always
earn the affection they crave. Harold Wilson, one of the
most skillful manipulators of the press, can still be as

paranoid as Richard Nixon, suspecting a plot under or between every line. Talking about himself in the third person, Wilson says, "The virulence with which the Labour leader is pursued by the Conservative press is out of all proportion to that against the Conservative leader." But at least Wilson's persecution mania is out in the open. On the left wing of his party there are more sinister ideas and men, like Anthony Wedgwood Benn, a doctrinaire *apparatchik*. Benn has called on the labor unions within newspapers "to see that what is said about us is true." Even without his encouragement, unions often threaten to shut down a paper unless it holds its tongue about their own activities. Industrial sabotage on the presses is frequent but unreported.

The press's endemic weakness is that it reflects the traditional deference of the British toward their institutions, and their awe of authority. Newspapers will far more readily do what they have been convinced is patriotic, even if it means keeping quiet. The editor of the *Financial Times,* for example, confessed that for two years he kept out of the paper any story hinting that sterling might be devalued, which it subsequently was. He now says he would never do it again, but the fact that an influential specialist paper can deliberately suppress bad news gives some measure of British editorial spunk. Jingoism and the pursuit of True Brit are stronger motives than skepticism, which often goes under the name of "knocking Britain." It is a case of the blind leading the blind.

6. THE LAW BY WHICH ALL LAW IS JUDGED

The Lion and the Flea and Other Stories

Of all those parts of the British idea which have been dispersed around the world, the English common law is still the most revered. Its hold has something of the aura of the holy tablets. Senator Sam Ervin, explaining the genius of the men who created the American Constitution, said, "So they went through all the great documents of the English law, from the Magna Carta on down, and whatever they found there they incorporated in the Constitution, to preserve the liberties of the people."

This kind of talk is resonant with the delusions of Anglophilia; the idea transcends the pragmatism of history as the tablet ennobles the chisel. Looking at the state of the English law now, Americans ought to feel as the

Greeks now do toward democracy—translations wear better than the originals.

The English courts have made asses of themselves and of the law. Unlike its brothers among the Custodians in Whitehall, the judiciary cannot conceal its hand or its incongruity. This is more than a breakdown in the law. The English Constitution is empirical: the safeguards it provides for civil rights are not endurable. They can be—and are—revised by government lawyers without reference either to Parliament or the judiciary. A capricious executive and a compliant—or worse, a sympathetic —judiciary can easily manipulate the machinery of the state to its own preference and convenience.

If it rests on anything, the reputation of English law rests on the concept of justice administered dispassionately, detached from and above the petty allegiances of men and self-serving motives. In reality, the courts are ritualistic and the law is overcomplicated, anachronistic, painfully slow, and far too expensive. Even worse, as the following case demonstrates, the judiciary is fierce in defense of the powerful and dilatory in defense of the weak.

Whiskey advertisements like to give the impression of a cottage industry, a rustic process in which the rare waters of Highland streams are transformed into a golden nectar by a race of men with canny noses and tight purses. Like most businesses that have seen a local demand turn into an international fashion, Scotch whiskey distillers trade on their tradition long after the realities of mass production have made their original plants museum pieces.

There still seems to be a healthy diversity of choice in the whiskey market: among the brands lining liquor-store shelves five of the most ubiquitous are Johnnie Walker, Haig, Dewar's, Black and White, and White Horse. In fact, all of these are produced by the same company. So are Vat 69, King George IV, and the rarer de luxe whiskeys like The Antiquary, Crawford's, and Talisker. So are Gordon's, the world's largest-selling gin, Booth's gin, High & Dry gin, Cossack vodka, and the staple of colonial sundowners, Pimm's Cups. The happy provider of all this inner warmth is the Distillers Company of Edinburgh and Glasgow.

The Distillers Company is the corporate extension of the Scottish character. It is wealthy, secretive, and prudent in its accounting, and most of its executives share a passion for the sport that the Scots invented, golf. But the company has more than traditional reasons for keeping a low profile. With 60 percent of the world market for Scotch whiskey and a stranglehold on the British liquor market, it is anxious not to attract the attentions of antimonopolists. Given Britain's supine view of monopoly, the company knows that it is safe as long as it keeps its nose clean.

Whiskey combines the two things that make it a dream business: a seemingly insatiable demand and exclusive resources that rule out imitations. By far the largest thirst for Scotch whiskey outside of Scotland is in the United States, which imported 25 million proof gallons of the stuff in 1972. Forty percent of the American market for Scotch is in the hands of the Distillers Company—about 30 percent of its total sales. Its pretax profit in 1973 was $175 million.

On the basis of this it might seem that the small and reticent band of men guiding the company should feel relaxed as they toast each other, with their own brands, at their boardroom lunches. But something has been bugging them; an intrusive beam of publicity has fallen across their affairs. It has nothing to do with whiskey or any of the other spirits they dispense. The public was in pursuit of the conscience of the Distillers Company, and it was proving harder to find than the oldest and rarest of the bonded Glenlivets.

In 1961 several British medical journals carried advertisements for a drug called Distaval, saying: "Distaval [thalidomide] can be given with complete safety to pregnant women and nursing mothers without adverse effect on mother and child." The makers of Distaval were a Distillers subsidiary, Distillers (Biochemicals) Ltd., which manufactured it under license from Chemie Grünenthal, a German company. Less than a month after the Distaval ads ran in Britain, the drug was withdrawn. A causal relationship had been established between thalidomide and deformities in children whose mothers had taken the drug during pregnancy.

In the United States, thanks to Dr. Frances Kelsey of the FDA, the only women who had taken thalidomide during pregnancy had done so as part of clinical trials. There were about twenty cases in America of deformed children. In Germany there were twenty-six hundred. And in Britain there were four hundred families faced with the nightmare of raising children lacking some or all of their limbs, and with other horrific deformities.

In November, 1962, the first writ alleging negligence by the Distillers Company was served by the father of a child born without arms. Ten years later, abstruse legal arguments—seemingly remote from the human tragedy —were still being played out in the British courts. The law had proved singularly confused and unrewarding for the parents. And the Distillers Company had been no more compassionate than the courts.

To have proved the drug manufacturers negligent in law would have been more straightforward if injury was caused after birth. The drug had done its damage at a point when British law did not recognize the victim as a living soul. Under American law there is a precedent covering the foetus; there is none in Britain. Because the foetus issue was "unsolved" in British law, the litigation bogged down on the issue of negligence. It was a formula for the kind of elegant procrastination that sends lawyers' fees on a binge, like an unstoppable taxi meter. There were thirty thousand documents from the Distillers files to be gone through. The action entered a timeless limbo. Some parents were advised that they had no case and could not sue; others thought it unnecessary to sue because Distillers would provide for them; many did not even know that their children were deformed by thalidomide because they didn't know the mother had taken the drug.

The mark on the children was obvious enough, but the burden on the parents became acute. Financial strains reduced some families to penury; psychological stress shattered previously ordered lives.

The first settlement by Distillers did not reach court until 1968. Only 58 of the children were involved. Their parents had been persuaded that to prove "a duty of care to a foetus," in the detached language of the lawyers, could not be guaranteed. Settlement was devised according to abject conditions. The counsel for the parents said he would accept 40 percent of whatever "normal liability for injury" was judged to be by the court. British law is so deficient in assessing damages for personal injury that the Law Commission, responsible for reform, says it lacks "any mathematical, actuarial, statistical, or other scientific basis." Not to mention something as abstract as compassion. The judge thought Distillers was very generous in its approach and said it would be "folly to refuse such an offer." The average sum per child worked out at $35,000. On an actuarial basis it would have been about $200,000.

To pacify the parents of another 374 victims, Distillers proposed a charitable trust fund amounting to just over $8 million. To each child this was worth $17,250, just over half the previous settlement. The parents were told by the lawyers that this compared "very favorably" with settlements in other countries. In Sweden the awards were worth about $125,000 per child; and in the United States, between $250,000 and $375,000.

The steel in the eye of Distillers began to show. The trust fund would be available only if *all* the parents agreed to it. When five held out, *their own lawyers* pressed them to settle, threatened that legal aid would be withdrawn, and made other minatory noises. They even tried to establish that the defiant parents were unacceptable as representatives of their own children's interests and to put their case in the hands of the official solicitor, who would presumably have joined the more compliant parents. When this case came to court, the whole Distillers case began slowly to unravel.

The Appeal Court ruled for the resisting parents. But before this the newspapers had begun to wake up to what was going on. "SCANDALOUS!" declared the *Daily Mail*. The day after, the paper got a letter from Kimber, Bull, the aptly named lawyers acting for the parents. The paper, said the lawyers, had committed a "clear contempt of court." The three words *contempt of court* have for years constituted the biggest booby trap in the path of campaigning editors, more intimidating than even the punitive libel laws. No comment was permissible on cases before the courts; any coverage at all if proceedings were "contemplated" was similarly sub judice. This was really Catch-22, since the only people to judge if a court case was imminent were the shadowy and often dilatory official prosecutors. If they said a case was "contemplated," nobody could prove otherwise. The letter from Kimber, Bull produced exactly the kind of situation where the law seemed at its worst.

It was technically true that the parents and the Distillers were involved in litigation, but the wrangling had gone on for so long—for most of the time out of court—that it could almost have been regarded as dormant. The details were so complex, and the lawyers so stricken with constipation, that there was little, if any, prospect of a case being brought to trial. In any event, the *Daily Mail* decided to call the bluff and ran a second story. What happened then involves a figure at the center of British law and its most questionable behavior. The attorney general intervend.

Although this was a civil, not criminal, action, and although no court was in session, the attorney general *appeared on behalf of Distillers*. He warned that a formal complaint had been made of contempt of court—but it had been made by Kimber, Bull who were acting on behalf of the parents, not the drug company! The *Daily Mail* was stopped in its tracks.

The office of the attorney general originated in the thirteenth century. Its function was to preserve the royal interests in court. Today he is one of the three "law officers of the crown." The other two are the solicitor general and, the most senior of the trio, the lord chancellor. They are political appointees and members of the government. The tradition is that attorneys general plead "no political motive," even in cases where a political motive would have seemed reasonable and rational—in, for example, the leakage of secrets. To regard their role as anything but ambivalent requires generous credulity.

Although this time Sir Peter Rawlinson, Edward Heath's attorney general, had gagged the press, its timidity was not to last. For several years the assiduous investigating team of *The Sunday Times* had been building up a file on Distillers and thalidomide. Late in 1972 *The Sunday Times* ran a three-page introduction to what it promised would be a definitive account. With only this trailer to go on, the attorney general materialized again, asking for an injunction to restrain publication of the second article—on behalf of Distillers. The paper allowed the attorney general to read the second article in draft and he decided that it would exert "undue pressure" on Distillers. Bearing in mind the harrowing and relentless pressure applied by the company on the parents to capitulate to its settlement offer, the right response would have been a hollow laugh.

But the judges of the High Court were more somber. They managed to disinter a precedent from 1742 to help establish that "the test of contempt is whether the words complained of create a serious risk that the course of justice may be interfered with." The writs in the thalidomide case had been issued *four years* earlier; the prospect of bringing the writs to court was not taken seriously. The preservation of the dignity and processes of the law was, apparently, more important than either the public interest or the children's.

The attorney general said his duty was "to mind generally the public interest, the fair administration of justice, and the interests of the court." The High Court decided that *The Sunday Times* story should be suppressed, but the Appeal Court did not agree. The case developed into a contest of learned nabobs.

In the Appeal Court, Lord Denning, something of a maverick on the bench, pointed out that the proposed Distillers Trust Fund represented little more than 1 percent of the profits of Distillers in the ten years since the tragedy. He found the attorney general's intervention strange, and he was critical of the lawyers: "These actions have gone soundly to sleep. . . . no one has awakened them. I think I can see why." But the attorney general was obdurate. When the Appeal Court ruled in favor of *The Sunday Times,* he went to the court of last resort, the House of Lords. After painfully slow deliberation, it supported the gag. But by that time the law's impotence was overtaken by events.

Throughout the whole saga the taciturn chairman of Distillers, Sir Alex McDonald, had avoided any public appearances or pronouncements. Distillers had long since sold its drug business to the American company Eli Lilly. Distillers had, in any case, prudently taken out insurance against claims from the public (one of the members of the Lloyds syndicate was Heath's minister of health, supposedly involved in the fate of the children; another Heath minister had been a lobbyist for Distillers).

Distillers was a tightwad in its own business. Apart from the directors, only one out of its nineteen thousand employees earned more than a four-figure (sterling) salary. The board was a mixture of beady-eyed accountants like McDonald, liquor technicians, and a few quasi-aristocratic whiskey-family heirs. There was also Henry Evelyn Alexander Dewar, third Baron Forteviot and the largest personal shareholder. The kilted Lord Forteviot lives in a castle surrounded by fifteen thousand acres of park. The estate is intersected by public roads, but the staff cut down bushes growing along the verge to discourage passing drivers from stopping to pick blackberries.

A stockbrokers' report described the Distillers board as "excessively secretive." The company's public demeanor was similar. Uproar over thalidomide in Parliament and the press seemed to the men in Scotland typical of hysteria in London, that flashy and dangerous city. In Edinburgh, McDonald, who looks like a bulkier version of Khrushchev, lives a simple social life. No Edinburgh magnate, so long as he stays there, needs to worry much about critical scrutiny by the Scottish newspapers, a servile and parochial bunch. And the Distillers shareholders, who got more than $61 million out of the company in 1972, were fat and happy. But it was through some of its shareholders that Distillers was finally led to its conscience.

The company is attractive to institutional investors wanting consistent earnings and guaranteed growth. Two insurance companies, the Prudential and the Brittanic, have between them nearly 4 percent of Distillers shares— a large enough portion to be influential, because of the dispersion of most holdings. Financial leverage is one thing, but moral influence has not been regarded as a congenital characteristic of large financial institutions.

Nevertheless, some of the shrewder lobbyists on behalf of the thalidomide parents, enraged by the persistent elusiveness of Sir Alex McDonald and his fellow directors, sought out these institutional shareholders. They were helped by some discreet political pressure. Distillers finally coughed up a new settlement worth seven times the original trust fund, involving $50 million, to be paid in installments over ten years, averaging about $135,000 for each child.

Ten years of legal shadowboxing had been fruitless; six months of a press campaign, although legally emasculated, had extracted the appropriate social response. A new sanction had been used against corporate intransigence, the leverage of the institutional shareholder. The clown of the story, if not the villain, was the law. Its performance left troubling inferences.

If corporate morality produced black comedy in the courts, sexual morality has been an equally unhappy test. In 1960 the British were finally allowed to read *Lady Chatterley's Lover*—thirty-two years after Lawrence wrote it. But the *Lady Chatterley* trial, for all its cathartic value, turned out to be a false dawn for literary and sexual license. It is a basic tenet of the British idea that sex is too dangerous to be enjoyed by peasants. "Is it the kind of book you would want your servants to read?" was the rubric of the crown's case against the publishers of *Lady Chatterley*. This attitude persists. The gyrations of the higher courts, faced with the challenge of the rampant penis, are inelegant, contradictory, and intemperate. There was, for example, the *Oz* case—the longest obscenity trial in English history.

Oz was a garish, incoherent underground magazine created by an Australian prankster called Richard Neville. There was a gleam in Neville's eye suggesting that his real purpose was to exact an Aussie's revenge on the Pommies, and that he planned to achieve it with an ingenious put-on, designed to lure the courts into an action that could only end in their being ridiculed. If so, it worked better than he could have dared to hope.

The trial of *Oz*, for an issue aimed at children, found in Judge Argyle the kind of stern Victorian hand that the Puritans yearned for. Displaying contempt for "expert" witnesses called by the defense, Argyle imposed two prison sentences, stiff fines, and—a final touch of the old colonialism—recommended that Neville should be deported, like the convicts who were the original involuntary settlers of British Australia.

These Draconian penalties were removed by the judges of the Appeal Court. But their lordships then became muddled over the meanings of "indecent," "obscene," "lewd," "filthy," and "repulsive." In the confusion, they put new constraints on publishers. They ruled that although a book could be judged as a whole, a newspaper or magazine could be offensive if any single article, illustration, or cartoon was ruled to be capable of "depraving or corrupting." The Appeal Court also disqualified the testimony of expert witnesses and made its minatory warning that prison sentences could be expected in future cases. Neville's flea aroused the lion, probably by biting its balls.

But some judges knew better how to avoid the trap of a direct cultural and political confrontation in court. The longest and most expensive trial in British legal history—lasting 110 days and producing three million words of evidence—was the Angry Brigade case. Eight young people, four men and four women, were accused of involvement in a wave of political bombings going back to 1968, producing one serious injury. The radical left braced itself for a show trial, like that of the Chicago Eight, in which martyrs would be made for the sake of an enraged middle class. The police were certainly hoping for the same thing.

In the event, the Old Bailey judge, Mr. Justice James,

managed to defuse the whole situation. He allowed the defense to reject thirty-nine jurors on political grounds; he allowed three of the accused to conduct their own defense; and he allowed great latitude in defense submissions, particularly to challenge police evidence. Four of the eight were jailed for ten years, the other four acquitted for reasons implying that the jury thought the police had planted evidence. The sentences were not light, but one of those who was acquitted admitted afterward:

> It was a victory for the judge, and for the tactics he adopted. He ran it very intelligently indeed. We could win against the prosecution, but we couldn't win against him, because he refused to take a class position. He insisted on remaining impartial, interpreting only the law and directing the jury to do the same.

The defendants were lucky, but so were the Custodians. A judge who had chosen to use the eight as an example, which in other hands might well have happened, would have roused British campus radicals from their congenital lassitude. The neanderthal British phobias were shown only too clearly by the way some of the more lunatic newspapers covered the Angry Brigade trial, asserting that the eight were typical of university students as pampered welfare cases and people with freakish sex lives.

The police came out less well than the judiciary. Their methods had been overmuscular and simpleminded. One defendant was held in custody for 472 days without trial, the equivalent of a two-year sentence with remission. The police complained that the law was weighted too far in favor of the defense and too little in favor of the prosecution. This view is the basis of a growing cleavage between the police and liberal lawyers. It was endorsed by a committee set up under a hawkish judge, Lord Justice Edmund Davies, to review criminal-law procedures.

The rights of a suspect under English law are already inferior to those in America. Interrogation inside police stations takes place without the presence of a lawyer or witnesses (hence the scope for "blooding"). The suspect can be detained for periods of time without access to a lawyer and without any charges being brought (even Spain is more liberal). There is a notorious method known as "the verbals" in which the police induce a statement and have the suspect sign it, in circumstances where intimidation is easy.

The Davies Committee wanted to erode the suspect's rights even more. It recommended the virtual abolition of the "right to silence," both under police interrogation and during trial; much wider admission of hearsay evidence; and the increased admissibility of evidence of any previous record on the accused. The police were delighted. Jurists were stunned, including some outside Britain who look to the British law as the one by which all others are judged. Doctor Manfred Simon, former president of a chamber of the Court of Appeal in Paris, says, "Any changes that would endanger the proper protection given by the English system to the accused is a matter of general, not merely English, concern."

The changes suggested by the Davies Committee would, said Dr. Simon, "introduce into English law certain features of the so-called inquisitorial procedure, as applied in France, without establishing at the same time safeguards comparable to those, imperfect as they may be, which have been inserted into French legislation with a view to protecting the accused."

Even more alarming to this foreign observer was that the changes suggested "the first timid attempt to dismantle the venerable fortress built by many generations of British lawyers to protect the innocent . . . a sad illustration of the insidious process whereby standards of even the most civilized countries can, under modern pressures, subtly but irresistibly be eroded."

Trial lawyers who appear both for the defense and prosecution refute the police case that things are loaded against them. Aware also of the increasingly dubious methods of the police, these lawyers rejected the Davies Committee's ideas and said:

> We would have expected the maintenance of safeguards for the individual against oppression or malicious or vindictive prosecution to have been at the very center of an inquiry . . . and this is the more so when public confidence in the police in some parts of the country is in question.

These lawyers want to move toward the American system, and as a further safeguard they want any statement made after the police have refused access to a lawyer to be declared inadmissible. But the really significant thing about the response of the trial lawyers is that they have, virtually en masse, emerged as the real libertarians, between a reactionary judiciary on the one hand and the police hard-liners on the other. The fissure is serious. It reveals not only a professional dispute but a political polarity. Lawyers do not lightly talk of "malicious or vindictive prosecution." If the criminal law is vulnerable to naked political pressures, the outcome could be catastrophic.

The political pressures have, if anything, been aggravated by an increasingly political instinct in the police hierarchy. At one time, whatever the sentiments of the top policemen, they were not inclined toward the subtleties of political lobbying. As late as 1972 the Association of Chief Police Officers submitted a memorandum to a government inquiry recommending the retention of the whole of the Official Secrets Act in such unambiguous terms ("journalists are prone to put forward a view that publication of official matters is in the public interest") that it was counterproductive. But the police have now gained a figurehead who is much more plausible.

Sir Robert Mark, the head of Scotland Yard and the commissioner of the Metropolitan Police, has shown skilled political footwork throughout his rapid rise to the top. Mark has been shrewd enough to secure his lines of communication with the Home Office (which is responsible for the police), and the degree to which he is now sanctioned as the social philosopher of the "law-and-order" lobby was shown in a remarkable lecture on BBC television. *The Times* was ready to rhapsodize over this performance as "excellent and lucid." But a more considered analysis of what he said, and the way he said it, is less reassuring.

Mark adopted the didactic simplicity of a policeman explaining the highway code to schoolchildren, and to create the right aura of complacency he made the usual reference to his own profession as "the most accountable and therefore the most acceptable police in the world." And although he got his largest headlines over an attack on "bent" lawyers (which showed more the degree of public naïveté than any revelatory value), Mark's most serious target was the jury system: "I cannot think of any other social institution which is protected from rational inquiry because investigation might show that it wasn't doing its job."

The essence of the police frustration with juries lies in the fact that half of the people who plead not guilty in front of juries are acquitted. "Every acquittal," said Mark, "is a case in which either a guilty man has been allowed to go free or an innocent citizen has been put to the trouble and expense of defending himself." And then, revealing his own conclusion, he said, "The proportion of those acquittals relating to those whom experienced police officers believe to be guilty is too high to be acceptable." But Mark failed to point out that, with the guilty pleas added, only a quarter of the defendants before the courts are acquitted.

If the efficacy of the law and the courts were to be

based on the instincts of "experienced police officers"—
and their assumption of the accused's guilt—things would
be going a lot further away from the historical presump-
tion of innocence than even the Davies Committee had
dared to propose. Mark's expression of the police resentment of transparently concocted defenses was understandable, but his lack of sensibility toward the fragile balance of the law makes his judgment very dubious.

Seen as a part of a calculated erosion of the rights of
the accused and the position of juries, Mark is another
polarizing influence in the battle between the bar and the
axis of the police and the legal Custodians. Without consulting either Parliament or practicing lawyers, the lord
chancellor agreed with the attorney general and the lord
chief justice that the right of defendants to know the occupation of jurors should be abolished. This information
had been important in the challenges made of jurors in
the Angry Brigade trial. Basic rights disappear with surprising ease.

With the ermine and scarlet, the silk robes, the wigs of
varied length according to pecking order, judges are
placed in ethereal remoteness. Why did the courts choose
to stay frozen in costume? Was it a subconscious yearning
for time to stand still while their dignity was complete,
their authority absolute? An eighteenth-century lawyer
could return today to a British court to find it—and the
law—thoroughly familiar. The precedents set in his time
are still dusted off and thought relevant to today's moral
dilemmas. Anachronism and insularity have become the
law's self-defense.

By making themselves absurd and irrelevant, the
courts have also made themselves vulnerable. Plainly
dressed despots have subverted the authority of the man
in fancy dress. There is now a growing body of law in
Britain that governs individual rights but has little, if anything, to do with the courts. It is the law of statute, made

not by lawyers but by administrators. It is made to suit the convenience of the machine, and the convenience of the machine is as yielding to the rights of the individual as is a brick wall to the fist of a man. The English common law, that anchor of the Anglo-Saxon concept of freedom, is crumbling under the infection of this new law.

The development of the law of statute has not been sudden. It has been in progress a long time and not particularly subtly or stealthily. As early as 1911 a senior English judge, Sir. H. H. Cozens-Hardy, warned:

> Administrative action generally means something done by a man whose name you do not know, sitting at a desk in a government office, very apt to be a despot if free from the interference of the Courts of Justice.

The encroachment of the courts by administrative statutes was already under way, but for worthy enough motives. Between 1905 and 1914, the first years of the welfare state, expenditure on the social services doubled. Even then most of the dealings between the state and the individual involved only the mailman or policeman. Paperwork was minimal. An Englishman didn't need a passport to travel. If he was prosperous enough, he was as free as a bird. World War I changed all that, and the freedoms surrendered then have never been won back.

By 1929 Lord Hewart, a bibulous judge, became so alarmed by the way the line between the executive and the judiciary was being blurred that he wrote a book called *The New Despotism*. Hewart saw the executive as the champions of "organized lawlessness," and produced a list of their basic precepts. The first three were:

1. The business of the executive is to govern.
2. The only persons fit to govern are experts.
3. The experts in the art of government are the permanent officials who, exhibiting an ancient and too much ne-

glected virtue, "think themselves worthy of great things, being worthy."

Hewart was incredibly prescient. These are precisely the arguments now used to defend the congenital furtiveness of the Custodians. Hewart saw that the cult of expertise would convince its followers that government "can be disposed of only if [the experts] were placed above Parliament and beyond the jurisdiction of the courts." Coming from somebody steeped in the social background of the Custodians, this prediction had certitude.

The seizure of law-making by the executive, unimpeded since then, has now taken a new direction. The legislation of the second stage of the welfare state, between 1945 and 1952, was, like the first, essentially paternalist. The new statutes are interventionist. The French *droit administratif* involves statutory laws with built-in judicial safeguards. The contemporary British version omits any similar restraints. Its most ardent architect so far is a strange hybrid of politician, lawyer, and empire builder called Sir Geoffrey Howe. Only in his mid-forties, Howe is the doctrinal lawyer of the corporate state. He created the divisive and unworkable Industrial Relations Act, the first attempt in British history to make labor unions answerable to a court. Not to any existing court, but to the Industrial Relations Court. This was a minor step compared to Howe's tour de force, the legislation amending the British system to the requirements of Common Market membership.

This change is progressive, eventually transferring fundamental rights to Brussels and the European bureaucracy. Howe therefore becomes as influential as the architects of the Magna Carta. Howe's law shows an affection for statutes and an impatience with courts. His laws are made in ministries. He drafted consumer-protection legislation giving sweeping powers to bureaucrats, leaving the courts as a last resort. It appears to be in a good cause, except that once again the ministry supposed to be a policeman is also the sponsor of most of the potential offenders—the Department of Trade and Industry. Howe's explanation is "You are not going to solve consumer grievances by mountains of litigation. But what you do is introduce more situations in which litigation is possible at the end of the road, and then this changes the whole atmosphere." It sounds as though the abstraction of "atmosphere," with its implied threat, is reckoned to be more useful than a court. A lawyer who sets up a bureaucracy to make law as it goes along, regarding courts only as a last resort, is a new kind of lawyer indeed.

As the old law is undermined, so too is its constitutional significance. Because it is unwritten, the English Constitution lives only in English law. Usurp that law, and you usurp the Constitution. The Custodians have seen the debility of the courts, and they have taken the law into their own hands.

The benign reputation of the British policeman has always rested to some extent on the belief that he is a bit dimwitted. The authors who helped to establish this legend took the middle-class view that gifted amateurs like Sherlock Holmes, Miss Marple, Lord Peter Wimsey, and even a priest like Father Brown were better detectives than pros. There is a strong streak of snobbery in this: in their manners and their accents the police have been presented as deferential proles. The "good copper" became a universal figure of both fun and respect. As late as 1971 *The New Yorker* magazine, a sort of emotional depository for Anglophilia, was able with conviction to run a profile of a London police constable as that same bicycle-riding, avuncular good Samaritan of fiction. To the inhabitants of Manhattan it was, of course, a calculated piece of escapism. Since they were living with a siege mentality in the midst of soaring crime rates and dependent on an openly corrupt police force, the confirmation that the good copper still existed must have increased the already steady migration of New Yorkers to London.

The most generous thing to be said about the *New Yorker* profile is that its timing was bad. About the time it appeared, London's allegedly impeccable police force was going through an unprecedented series of scandals. The rot came out into the open because of the purging zeal of a new police chief. At the same time a market-research study revealed that half the adult population and two-thirds of the younger people were sufficiently disenchanted with the police to feel more fearful of them than respectful. Although the study's results were suppressed (ironically, it was commissioned to aid police recruiting), the shift in attitudes was obvious and irretrievable.

The seriousness of the fall of the good copper is still relative. Other countries assume that their police are corrupt, trigger-happy, brutal toward dissent, and immune to reform. These traits are now at least visible in the British police, but so far they indicate a problem rather than an epidemic. Because the legend of incorruptibility was so strong, its collapse comes as a shock.

At the heart of the legend is Scotland Yard, controlling the twenty thousand men of the Metropolitan Police. Things have gone wrong at the Yard. Two of its elite units, the Flying Squad and the Drugs Squad, were decimated by corruption charges. The *known* rate of corruption in the London police is 1 percent—incredibly low by New York standards, but a disaster measured against the British tradition. In 1972 the number of policemen in London who admitted offences doubled, to 144. Eighty were, to use the official euphemism, allowed to "retire early."

The Yard was too ready to believe its own propaganda. The special squads developed into jealously preserved substates of their own. Organization and methods fell behind the more sophisticated developments in crime. Interdepartmental fights raged. The most intransigent group, the huge Criminal Investigation Department (CID), was corrupted but self-policing, so that men who fell under suspicion could be shunted out of sight to another division rather than indicted. The straight police were demoralized by this kind of license, and by the arrogant unscrupulousness of some of the leadership.

Sir Robert Mark was put into the Yard to sort it out. For two years the old units fought to keep their identity and autonomy, a kind of star system dependent more on custom than achievement. But Mark dismantled the monolithic CID, and as a first step in matching the system to the crimes, he set up a bank-robbery unit that had early, spectacular successes. The Flying Squad, proudest of all the old units, survived only in name. It became a two-hundred-man "strategic force." Because certain types of crime, like truck hijacking, were among the most apparent British contributions to the Common Market, another unit was formed to coordinate with European police. There was a new intelligence system based on the constant surveillance of "target" criminals.

All these reforms have improved efficiency but caused a great deal of disenchantment among the old guard. What the reforms can't do is make the police any more loved. And in the precarious relationship between the good copper and the British public, no issue is more sensitive than whether or not the policeman should carry a gun. Rather than face this dilemma squarely, the police have now drifted to a point where their options are few—tacitly the London police is already an armed force.

British criminals once abhorred the firearm as the sign of an unprofessional and unstable temperament. This attitude is still prevalent among small fry, but the new, highly organized and mobile gangs with targets like banks and bullion shipments face determined resistance in which only guns are decisive. And since the young hit men have taken to using amphetamines to boost their nerves, an unarmed copper is desperately and increasingly vulnerable.

The British police have practiced 140 years of self-denial in the argument of whether or not to meet arms with arms. The idea of cops and criminals shooting it out in city streets is alien to the British experience. In Australia, which takes many of its habits and traditions from Britain, the police resorted to guns, with the result that they face a much more violent crime war. In Britain the compromise has been, without any open assent or debate, to limit the arms either to an anticipated need, or to special units trained in their use. In 1970 the police were issued guns on 1,072 occasions; by 1972 the figure had more than doubled. And at the end of that year, by the kind of coincidence that was sooner or later inevitable, there was the first public shoot-out.

An armed copper on his way to guard a London embassy walked right into a bank raid. One of the gang fired at him with a shotgun; simultaneously the copper fired back, fatally wounding the raider. This incident revealed the existence of Scotland Yard's Special Patrol Group, which patrols in unmarked vehicles. It includes forty men who regularly carry guns. In this episode the public's sympathy was with the police, but a month later the same unit was involved in a less impressive action.

Two armed Special Patrol Group men faced three young Pakistanis staging a political protest at the Indian High Commission. The Pakistanis were brandishing guns and refused to surrender. The SPG men fired eleven shots, all but one of the rounds in their guns. Two of the Pakistanis were killed. Their "guns" were toys sold in Woolworth at $1.25 each. The Pakistanis probably believed the legend that British cops would not shoot to kill. It was the judgment of a matter of seconds, not easy on each side, but the bluff was fatal. SPG men carrying .38 Smith and Wesson revolvers, each with six rounds in the magazine and another six at the ready, are a new phenomenon. A line has been crossed; there is no going back.

Asian community leaders wondered whether the police would have been quite so trigger-happy if the raiders had been white. It is an understandable question. After the firearms debate, the most critical issue in the social role of the British police is their attitude toward blacks. The record is bleak. Researchers have found that in the mind of the good copper colored people are "permanently in the area of suspicion." In one sense, the police role in race relations is thankless. The police are regarded by the blacks (particularly those born in Britain) as the most immediate agents of a society that has cheated them. The good copper is the target for grievances for which he is not to blame. But there is no doubt that the average copper reflects the racial attitudes of his own class, and most coppers have working-class backgrounds. "Have you been to a wog house?" asks a typical copper. "They stink, they really do smell terrible."

In the absence of adequate and trained community servants, the police are expected to be social workers of great sensitivity when faced with racial problems. Yet their preparation for this role, even supposing they accept it, has been minimal. The police policy is muddled and ambivalent. In one West Indian neighborhood in London the police had some success with an exercise to explain themselves to the blacks. But only weeks later, with no apparent provocation, the Special Patrol Group descended on the same area and began frisking blacks in the street, completely negating the public-relations effort.

In Liverpool, a city with a history of successive migrations of Irish, Scots, Chinese, West Indians, and Asians, a courageous policewoman went on BBC radio to expose this story:

> In certain police stations, particularly in the city center, brutality and drug planting and harassing of minority

groups takes place regularly. I witnessed a police sergeant attack a teen-age youth who had reported to the station on parole. The sergeant poured insults on the youth, picked him up by the coat lapels and banged his head against the wall several times, before throwing him into a chair. The youth was then dragged out to a police jeep and driven away. After hearing the word "agriculture" used on a number of occasions I asked what it meant. The reply was—"planting, but you can leave that to us."

This might be music to the ears of extreme-right-wing agitators like the National Front, whose literature attributes all violent crime to blacks, but every piece of evidence of this kind—and there are many—discredits the police both as the glue in society and as the agents of the law. In truth, the crime rate among blacks is no higher than among whites, and in many immigrant communities—particularly Asian—it is substantially lower. The chief constable of Leeds, for example, says, "Immigrant areas are less of a problem to us than the skinheads or the crombies" (two brands of white teen-age thug). These salient statistics are buried under white prejudice; both the courts and the media build up frightening images of black muggers without bothering to check the facts.

An obvious palliative would be the recruitment of black policemen. But this has been studiously neglected. The first black copper did not appear until 1965. By 1972 there were still fewer than forty—0.043 percent of the total police force. One West Indian copper in London says, "When you join the force you keep your friends and lose your acquaintances." The suspicion is so heavy that a black in uniform feels like an Uncle Tom. As one black community leader puts it, "I could not see myself becoming part of an institution that in every respect seems to be bent on keeping us down and molesting us."

As the trust of the public in the police ebbs away, the police cover their tracks effectively. For most complaints against police conduct they act as their own judge and jury. Only allegations of criminal misconduct are referred outside, and then to the director of Public Prosecutions, who is closely connected to the police, rather than to an independent scrutineer. In 1971 there were 4,314 complaints against the London police alone. Only 145 were acted upon. Blacks have found it impossible to be heard. Out of 37 cases sifted from 155 complaints made to the Jamaican High Commission, not one was said to have any substance.

Attempts to put the complaints procedure into independent hands have met a stone wall. A review carried out by the police themselves was never published. Another attempt in 1973 was deflected when the government offered a "study." The idea this time is a version of that Scandinavian fashion, the ombudsman, already cynically devalued in Britain. This version would even lack the power to call for papers and witnesses. He would be a "last resort," to review the reviewers who would be . . . you guessed it, the police. Meantime, complaints against the London police are rising by nearly 30 percent a year.

In 1829, when Colonel Charles Rowan and Richard Mayne created the first police force, their priority was the simple nineteenth-century one of protecting life and property and, as they put it in their first manifesto, "the preservation of public tranquillity." The London of the nineteenth century could be as dangerous and as squalid as the New York of the 1970s. The copper kept clear of politics, and social pressures were no part of his concern. His achievement was to create that "public tranquillity" by pacifying the streets. He is falling from grace now as both the social pressures intensify and criminals become much smarter.

The most celebrated heist of all time, the 1963 Great Train Robbery, can now be seen as the closing episode in the old-style British crime war. Apart from an unplanned and brutal knock on the head for the train's engineer, the robbers observed the gentleman's agreement of no vio-

lence and polite dialogue. Their victim was socially redeeming: the big banks. And the ingenuity of their planning reflected the highest Boy Scout/Commando standards. To catch them, the police used the traditional
method of a dogged and systematic manhunt by men
who were familiar with the character and habits of the
criminals, just as it always was in the best of the Scotland
Yard fiction. There was even a classic dénouement: the
elusive fugitive who is nearly caught but finally gets away
somewhere into the palm trees of the South Pacific. Everything about the Great Train Robbery was human. Except the thirty-year sentences handed down by the judge,
reflecting more the position of banks in the social priorities of the Custodians than the damage of the crime. But
by then the face of crime had changed.

In London there was a transitional period when the
criminals turned very nasty. Two gangs, the Richardsons
in south London and the Krays in the northeast of the
city, spilled blood readily. The Krays were the more vi-
cious and the more flagrant. They gate-crashed London
high society and were briefly feted as "frightfully amusing." Their protection rackets controlled large tracts of
the West End. A trail of underworld assassinations
cleared their progress. But their work became uncomfortably visible. Scotland Yard had to form a special unit
to deal with them. The psychopathic twin gangsters, Ronald and Reginald Kray, were jailed for life. (They still
operate some of their old businesses from a prison cell
equipped with color TV.)

The Richardson gang favored the torture of nailing
dissidents to the floor through their kneecaps. They were
also rounded up and jailed. Both gangs had exposed the
divisional rigidity of Scotland Yard. They were dealt with
only by employing the special units. Although their crude
violence made them too visible, both the Krays and the
Richardsons had begun to realize that sophisticated swindles were more profitable, and more secure, than butch-

ery. The Krays dabbled in corporate fraud, international networks, and the use of legitimate "front" businesses. But they were too much infected, in manner and style, with the tradition of Bill Sykes and the old Cockney underworld to adapt in time.

While Sir Robert Mark's reorganized Scotland Yard is more effective in dealing with organized "blue-collar" crime, it is weak and ill-equipped to deal with the smart new crimes of the executive suite. The men of the Yard's Fraud Squad are recruited from the general ranks of the police force, remote from the subtleties of international corporate crime. The squad itself is divided between Scotland Yard and a section in the City of London financial district. Disputes between the two are compounded by the existence of another inspectorate at the Department of Trade and Industry, this time composed of civil servants. The known rate of company fraud in London is about $125 million a year, but the real figure is probably much higher because the game is so easy.

With the police hierarchy under Mark becoming more political, with their heavy-handedness in political cases and their widespread covert surveillance to support the apparatus of the secretive executive, and with the provocations of racial tension and smarter criminals, the old image of the congenial copper is already dead. Of all the fallen idols of Britain, this may well be the most serious casualty.

II. THE MISADVENTURES OF GREAT BRITAIN LTD.

7. REPLACING EMPIRE

Life at the Court of the Corporate Camelot

We are a world power and world influence or we are nothing.

—PRIME MINISTER HAROLD WILSON, 1964

Television soap operas are an infallible guide to a country's fantasy life. In Britain they are nearly always nostalgic: a quasi-Kipling series on the army in India at the
peak of empire; stiff-upper-lip escapes from Colditz Castle in World War II; the suicidal heroism of the RAF's
"Pathfinder" squadrons. Even documentaries follow the
same theme: mammoth reconstructions of World War II,
biographies of the great battle commanders. There is
nothing obscure about the appeal of these programs—
they all hark back not only to a time when Britannia

ruled the waves but also (and perhaps more significantly) to a time when the country was temporarily pulling together and, undoubtedly, at its most determined.

For a while in the 1960s this backward-looking trend was broken. A new fantasy won peak-time television success: the thrills of big business. A series called *The Power Game,* with a megalomaniac anti-hero called John Wilder, managed to make the aerospace industry look sexy. Wilder stood for the kind of leadership that the British wanted to believe in. He was a usurper of the old order making it big—the phallic airplanes he produced looked remarkably like the Concorde. Toward the end of the series Wilder was given a knighthood and slipped off his leash into Whitehall, like a wild dog into a chicken coop. It was a metaphor for what was supposed to be happening to the country. As that hope collapsed, so the TV series ended its run.

The life cycle of *The Power Game* was a paradigm of the formative years of the British corporate state. Turning the country from a colonial to a commercial power passed from fantasy to fiascos like the development of the Concorde. From the beginning, True Brit permeated the thinking:

> We are embarking on an adventure of the kind that enabled merchant venturers of the City of London and other cities in time past to win treasure and influence and power for Britain. We go forward in the same spirit of enterprise today. I believe the tide is right, the time is right, the winds are right. . . .

The winds? That was Harold Wilson, at the lord mayor's banquet in the City of London in 1966, four days after he had decided to try to negotiate Britain's entry into the Common Market.

It might seem a strange philosophy for a Socialist to produce, in the bearpit of British capitalism. His "merchant venturers" were unprincipled buccaneers, later exalted as patriots, who pillaged the wealth of the Indies under the British flag. This didn't much matter: they were sanctified by legend, and the British live off their legends. Wilson is prone to such generous interpretations of the past; from an early age he showed deep allegiance to the British idea. At the age of twelve he won a newspaper competition for describing, in less than one hundred words, his hero. His choice was Baden-Powell. He likes the operas of Gilbert and Sullivan, and in his family album there is a picture of the young Wilson dressed as a naval officer for a walk-on role in *H.M.S. Pinafore.* Later, as prime minister, he had a predilection for holding conferences on warships. To him the national heritage is much as portrayed by his favorite historian, the jingoistic Sir Arthur Bryant: a pageant full of gilded and heroic figures.

Now a new race of folk heroes was in the making, the knights of the corporate Camelot. Wilson played Merlin, summoning the genie of technology from the cave and offering it to the tired nation as a restorative. To bring this off, there had to be a somersault in social and political attitudes. The Whitehall view of business was like that of the landlord of a whorehouse: it was useful for filling the pockets, but not something you talked about. So it was traumatic for the Custodians to be told that with the empire gone they had better learn the language of the hard sell. It was like trying to turn a spinster into a topless go-go girl.

From 1964, under first Wilson's Labour regime and then Edward Heath's Conservative government, the Custodians have been forced into the embrace of big business. The national interest and the corporate interest have been fused. The traditional separation of government and business has been deliberately dismantled, and the boundaries are now obscured. But it is a contract between two inimical psyches, the ascetic and the venal. It is also often a contract between two kinds of incompetence:

otiose bureaucracy and congenitally sloppy management. To create this axis between business and government, there has been an unparalleled bureaucratic growth. Between 1965 and 1971 the whole structure of Whitehall changed. In 1965 there was one dominant department in the center, the Treasury, and nineteen subject ministries. By 1971 there was a new three-tier system. At the top, the power of the Treasury had been dispersed into three units, the sum greater than the parts: a Civil Service Department as the administrative focus; the Cabinet Office in an expanded form; and the vestigial Treasury. Instead of diminishing the grasp of the Custodians by ending the monolithic role of the Treasury, this system made the political and administrative links even more arcane, especially in the Cabinet Office.

There was an equally portentous development in the second tier, the creation of three megaministries, the Department of Trade and Industry; the Department of the Environment; and the Department of Health and Social Security. Between them these three have a staff of 170,000. They have eclipsed the old "imperial" departments, the Foreign Office and the Defence Ministry. They also overshadow the third tier of minor ministries.

This concentration of power evolved through a bewildering chain reaction of departmental title changes and mergers. Officials controlling complex and accident-prone projects were shunted like nomads from one organizational chart to another. Each time, the line of command became more evanescent.

The same trend was axiomatic in British business. Conglomeration was the fashion, enthusiastically endorsed in Whitehall. By 1970 half of the net national output came from the hundred largest manufacturing firms (the top one hundred American companies produce only a third). On that trend, 90 percent of the nation's business would be in the hands of the top one hundred companies by the year 2000. Already just 9 percent of British industry accounts for 94 percent of all corporate trading profits. A concentration of business power like this would be unthinkable even in the homeland of the giant corporations. The U.S. Federal Trade Commission estimates that if a market could be regulated so that its four largest producers shared no more than 40 percent of that market, retail prices in those products could be cut by at least a quarter. In Britain there are more than 150 markets where 50 percent or more of the business is in the hands of one firm or group.

Between 1966 and 1968, the seminal period in government-sponsored mergers in Britain, the money spent per year in takeovers jumped from $1,267 million to $5,780 million. Both the creation of corporate giants and that of the Whitehall megaministries reflect the same idea: bigness equals clout. If Britain was not to be emasculated in the international markets, it had to be able to shape up to the giants. But this presupposed two things: that a correct choice would be made of the right businesses to be in, and that there was a supply of the management skills to carry it off. Both assumptions were wrong. The most direct result of the cult of bigness was that the mistakes got bigger.

To try to compensate for the inadequacy of the Custodians, specialist businessmen were drafted into Whitehall. These men were appalled by what they found. The ministry buildings, most of them monuments built at the peak of empire, were, like their inhabitants, marooned out of their time. Some had become grandiose slums. On the walls were murals of rampant True Brit, panoramas of imperial conquest. Yet the washrooms were so primitive that senior staff could be seen walking the corridors carrying their own private towels and soap, kept furtively from thieving hands in locked desk drawers, along with secret files.

This petty, spinsterish hoarding of things like soap and the cookies to go with afternoon tea is imbued in the

Whitehall mentality. One oil company executive, after a spell as an adviser, recalls, "The financial system dates back to Samuel Pepys. It was designed to stop kings spending money on mistresses."

Under the elaborately formalized mannerisms was a feline talent for in-fighting. A stiletto could be planted in the back with surgical precision and the victim could never tell, from those saturnine faces, where it had come from. Jealous of their power, assured by their illusions, and hostile to the intruding professionals, the Custodians sabotaged, neutralized, or bypassed the attempts to implant a grasp of modern management. A whole department set up by Wilson to provide the economic expertise the Treasury lacked had to be abandoned after the Custodians froze it out. Nothing could have been a clearer expression of the power of their club: either the game was played by their rules or it was not played at all. No matter that the rules were obsolete.

The outsiders were beaten by the ruthless use of negative power. Positive decision-making, especially on anything innovative, was too conspicuous and too perilous to careers depending on the automatic and secure pecking order of seniority. Lord Balogh, one of the outside advisers who had tried persistently to blow the whistle on the North Sea oil policy, commented ruefully, "Sins of commission are feared. The deadly vice of omission gets further promotion."

The rigid elitist breeding of the Custodians prejudices them against the character and style of the brasher businessman. The preference in Whitehall, if outsiders have to be tolerated, is for men who appear to reflect the Custodians' own values—as near as possible, the public servant rather than the individualist. In over a decade of attempted transplants, only one really has conspicuously "taken," and that, significantly, is from the same blood group. In an attempt to monitor the performance of the Custodians, Heath installed a "think tank" (Kennedyesque terms are still fashionable in Whitehall). And to run it he chose one of the few men in business who could appear to be playing the game by the rules of the Custodians, since he was virtually one of them himself: Victor, the third Baron Rothschild.

Unlike the French branch of the family, the British Rothschilds have a liberal bent. After wartime service in military intelligence, Victor Rothschild ran the research department at Shell Oil. He is a natural scientist, banker, polymath—and very superior person. In the high noon of Whitehall he could outdraw and outshoot the most mendacious mandarin. And the way he went about re- cruiting his staff of fifteen great thinkers is a classic ex- ample of tapping the elitist conduit. Rothschild has de- scribed it with candor: "I sometimes go to the Barbados, and since Dick Ross told me he knew a very good man on one of these sugar boards called Hector Hawkins, I made it my business to have rum punch with him—perhaps two—and I thought Hector was very nice and very good, so I asked if he would make a sacrifice and join me in the Cabinet Office."

The scene is pure Somerset Maugham: the porch at sundown, the colonial sugar plantations, the clink of ice in the tall glasses, the casual assessment of character as the punch warms the stomach, the value system of "very nice and very good." As one of the transactions of True Brit it is better than fiction. Somebody not in the know would have said—and it would have been a lack of couth fatal to his chances—"Barbados," not "*the* Barbados."

Lord Rothschild said that he had chosen another member of the think tank, the son of a fellow peer, "be- cause his father's a friend of mine and I asked his father if he might like it." With that kind of grapevine working for it, the think tank easily ingratiated itself into the sys- tem. It gave the Custodians no trouble, for it was a mir- ror of themselves.

One way of trying to make insiders out of outsiders is

to give them a title. Peerages and knighthoods are seldom given for selfless duty to the crown, more often for services rendered. Brasher businessmen are shamelessly importuning, especially if they are colonials. The Canadian owner of the London *Times,* Roy Thomson, embarrassed his editors by his abject supplications to Harold Macmillan, but in the end he got a peerage for being brave enough to save *The Times* from bankruptcy.

In 1966 Harold Wilson told a friend (later to be a baroness), "I hope in the next week or two to abolish the whole political honors system. . . . I don't know whether my colleagues will agree." Evidently they didn't. Wilson became profligate with his patronage. Where the Tories dispensed titles in return for donations to party funds, Wilson handed them out to the new folk heroes of Britain. He founded the court of the corporate Camelot.

A typical candidate was Donald Stokes, a man with the charmless smile of a car salesman, which is what he is. Stokes was picked by Wilson as the man to rationalize the foundering British auto industry. The American-owned satellites of Ford and GM were eating away the markets of undercapitalized` British dynasties turning out junk. Under Wilson's patronage, Stokes carried out a shotgun marriage of the old marques like Austin, Morris, Rover, Jaguar, Daimler, and Leyland. This ragbag became British Leyland, and Stokes got first a knighthood and then a peerage. He also got a continuing headache.

Under Wilson and Heath, corporate knighthoods and peerages showered into boardrooms. In every honors list there are an average of ten corporate knighthoods. At the summit of Camelot it doesn't stop with a simple peerage. Lord Cole, a frozen-food tycoon, became a Knight Grand Cross of the Order of the British Empire for a particularly painful act in the service of Britain: the plucking from the ashes of Rolls-Royce.

But these politically donated titles cannot buy admission to the inner sanctums of the Custodians. One of the most ruthless company surgeons, an exemplar of his order, is Sir Arnold Weinstock. His charisma bewitched two prime ministers, who sponsored his company, General Electric (unconnected with its American namesake) through a series of mergers to become the ninth largest in Britain, with a pretax profit of $231 million.

Weinstock is a Jew, which, together with his contempt for the traditional British style of doing business, loads the dice against him in places where the old guard rules. He was nominated by friends for membership of Brooks's Club in St. James's, one of the original cells of Custodian power, founded in 1764. These clubs use an anonymous method of voting to select new members: white balls placed in a box. If one or more black balls appear in the box the applicant has been "blackballed," a symbolic rejection with particularly unsubtle implications. Brooks's, a fortress of white supremacy, rejected Weinstock. It was not ready to accept the scourge of the British way of doing things. Among nearly a hundred peers of the realm who are members of Brooks's is Lord Lambton, drummed out of the House of Commons for sexual indiscretions but not from this citadel of selective tolerance.

Knighthoods—and acceptance into the clubs—fall as an automatic right to the Custodians in Whitehall once they reach senior rank. As Snow said of Hector Rose, they might not mean much outside, but they are a perquisite of office earned simply by seniority and kept for life, whatever fiascos follow in their wake. Whitehall knights look with disdain on the dilution of their order by the corporate Camelot. There is no way of gate-crashing their fortress, even if the outer battlements are not what they were.

And so there is this immutable cleavage between two cultures, supposedly joined in the contract to repackage Britain but fundamentally living in separate worlds according to inimical codes. Unwittingly, the ambit of the Custodians has been enlarged to a degree that is barely comprehended. Incompetent power is as dangerous as irresponsible power—perhaps it is even more dangerous, because it might always precipitate the kind of collapse for which, as Baroness Sharp warned, others are waiting in the wings. Her warning is not fanciful.

Between 1968 and 1970, the nadir of that Wilson regime, a cabal of disenchanted businessmen met frequently to consider a putsch. They had for a while the tacit support of two newspaper proprietors, Cecil King of the left-wing *Daily Mirror* (circulation 4.5 million) and Lord Thomson of *The Times* (circulation 400,000). This group never really coalesced into an organized threat, but its existence indicates how readily British businessmen believed that politics is too serious a business to be left to politicians. Among its number were the chairmen of the second- and fourth-ranking industrial giants, Shell and Imperial Chemical Industries; two peers from the outer nonexecutive fringes of the Custodians, the Lords Crowther and Shawcross; Lord Cole, chairman of Unilever, the fifth-ranking firm; and a recording-company tycoon.

Their choice for prime minister (without public consent) was Lord Robens, chairman of the nationalized coal industry and a favorite in the court of the corporate Camelot. *The Times* called for a coalition government, an idea with disastrous precedents. Secretly the businessmen's cabal used the term "emergency government." There was something wacky about the plot. It represented strong business clout but a great deal of political naïveté. Its planning was gauche, more sure of what was going wrong than of how to put it right. And there was one essentially right-wing conviction behind it: the British way was in jeopardy not because of the Custodians but because of industrial anarchy.

The history of industrial relations was appalling, but as culpable as the unions were the sloppy managements of the League of Gentlemen and the maladroit work of the Custodians. The putative coup faded away, ending with a desultory lunch at Brown's Hotel in 1970. Lord Crowther, who was then chairman of the Royal Commission on the British Constitution, said dolorously that he saw no future for British democracy, nor could he tell what would take its place.

In fact, the Constitution had already been preempted. The marriage of government and business, with the accretion of Custodian power that followed it, has swept away the checks and balances and severely diminished individual rights and freedoms. It has also created a divisive conflict between the old and the new styles of doing business.

8. BUSTING UP THE LEAGUE OF GENTLEMEN

The Hustlers, the Strippers,
and the Importance of Not Being Wet

The British dislike that Teutonic streak which makes a good corporate hatchet man. This is not to say that they are not themselves tricky. But they will seldom turn a crooked hand to the service of anything so impersonal as the body corporate. It is self that they serve best—though they would have you believe anything but. This helps to explain a common confusion in the minds of foreigners who get tangled with the British businessman: how can guys with such fancy footwork get the country into such a hell of a mess? Surely all that cunning ought to pay off? It does, but only for them.

The ambition of the British businessman has a low cut-off point. Having made enough money for his own comfort, he is content to coast along in a halfhearted way.

He assembles his perquisites: the company car, the chauffeur, the country cottage, the golf-club membership, a boat, and the numerous smaller luxuries of the expense account—all the symbols of success. He does not, beyond this, flourish his wealth or tax his energies. For an average member of the League of Gentlemen, this life is his ceiling.

He will look with distaste at corporate gangsterdom on the ITT scale, not because of the means but because of the ends. The British gentleman is best at being a privateer, not a hired hand. He has his own opaque code, which can be summarized as "It takes one to catch one; as long as we stick together, nobody gets caught."

Although the running of many large industrial firms has passed from the founding dynasties into the hands of managers answerable to shareholders, this has not altered the British belief that company directors need only to belong to the League of Gentlemen to qualify. More than two-thirds of British business executives went to a public (private) school. Eton still provides the largest number of future bankers, and 80 percent of the directors of major banks are the products of Oxbridge—exactly as they were in 1939. This is more important for the molding of their persona than for providing relevant skills. Only 8 percent have been to a business school, and only 35 percent have any professional qualification.

As a career with the Custodians is a birthright of the cream of the Oxbridge classics scholars, so a place in a British boardroom is regarded as the birthright of the less brilliant pupils, the members of the League of Gentlemen. There is also the question of nepotism. Despite the advent of the managers, nearly a third of the top 120 public companies in Britain have boards loaded with members of the founding family, or are under the patriarchal control of their creators. Even more decisive is the continuing grip of the old money on the financial springs of British business. Twenty-six of the twenty-seven largest financial institutions are run by men connected with each other by family, sixteen of them through "nuclear" family—siblings and parents, mostly brothers. Eight families are at the heart of this system, representing the classic elitist minority and one of them, the Barings, constitutes five different lines of the peerage. This combination of surviving dynasties and executives chosen according to their old school ties presents a stiff resistance to anyone believing that a business school and professional training are enough to earn a place at the top.

It was this system that the knights of the corporate Camelot were supposed to break. They had little chance. The gentlemen are as deeply entrenched in their citadel as are the Custodians. But what a different kind of citadel it is.

The City of London, the financial center since the first merchants and bankers set up business there centuries ago, is the most lawless square mile in the country. It is virtually a nation-state on its own, with its own lord mayor, its own police force, its own clubs, and its own ancient rituals and modern rackets. As a financial center its influence outstrips that of the country itself. It has more securities listed and a higher market capitalization than all other European markets put together. But it has never been a paragon of financial behavior.

City bankers invented swindles on a global scale. They created the South Sea Bubble in which a prime minister, Walpole, bought in at 130, sold at 1,000, and watched thousands ruined as the chimera collapsed. By the morals of the eighteenth century, this was unexceptionable. "Bribery in all its forms," noted an observer, "was as necessary in public affairs as are shells in war." This belief lives on, though the methods are now much more sophisticated. About the only area of modern technology that the League of Gentlemen have happily embraced is the corporate swindle. Like the furtive pact of sodomy in the public school dormitory, dirty tricks in the

City enjoy a tacit consent as part of the way of life—so long as nobody blabs.

The line between ethics and crime in British business has always been hazy. The ethos of the club prefers the loose and unwritten codes rather than open and explicit policing, self-regulation rather than imposed law. This springs directly from the double standard of the class system: gentlemen can be trusted, others need laws.

Many a large business has disreputable origins, whether it is a liquor fortune built out of bootlegging, or nineteenth-century social crimes like sweated child labor. After their early delinquent phase, the smart operators learn to cover their tracks and build an ivory tower for the next generation. In the City of London, one generation's bandits beget the next generation's pillars of society; the parvenu melts into the paragon. This requires a high degree of cynicism and hypocrisy, and the British are not underprovided with either.

As long as the compact of the League of Gentlemen holds together, it guarantees succession from one generation to another, hoarding the wealth and concealing the methods of gaining it. Nobody else need apply.

At the age of thirty-two, James Derrick Slater was having a touch of bad luck. Rising fast as the wheeler-dealer sales director under the as-yet-unknighted Donald Stokes, Slater had been selling trucks to Spaniards when he was struck down by a virus. The taut, driven Slater was no gentleman; he worked too hard and he had needed something to slow him down. The bug did it.

For convalescence, Stokes ordered him to the seaside resort of Bournemouth, a place where the genteel spend their twilight years being wheeled in bath chairs along the cliffs, wrapped in tartan rugs. It was a boring place for a hot-shot sales director to be stuck in. As a diversion, Slater started looking at stockbroker reports on public companies. Then came the Message. Some companies seemed to Slater curiously undervalued, often because their assets were marked down artificially low. And companies recuperating from losses were, he thought, revalued far too slowly by the market.

Slater decided to parlay his personal insight into a new kind of alchemy. The Message begat the System. In savings he had a modest $5,000. In one year the System turned the $5,000 into $125,000 by astute buying of undervalued stocks. It was a better way of making money than selling trucks. Magnanimously, Slater had let some of his friends in on the System. It ran so well that, to the great regret of Stokes, he set up business on his own as an investment adviser.

Slater had done more than find a way of getting rich quick. He had spotted the vulnerability of the League of Gentlemen. In his first year as a loner he made another $190,000. But that was only a beginning.

Slater was noticed by a London evening newspaper, which included him in a series of profiles of rising young businessmen. Another operator selected by the paper was an insurance broker called Peter Walker, three years younger than Slater.

Walker and Slater both left school at sixteen. Neither had any of the gloss of the League of Gentlemen. Slater's father was a builder, Walker's a grocer. Both came from north London suburbs and had flat suburban accents. But there was a difference in outlook. Walker had strong political ambitions and was in a group of young Tories who wanted to move their party off the grouse moors and into modern devices. Slater had the kind of Tory sympathies of anyone who suddenly has capital to conserve, but he was a monomaniac, in the grip of his own discovery. Nonetheless, Slater and Walker were as predestined as partners as Proctor and Gamble.

Their connection came when Walker organized a dinner for all the go-getters featured by the evening paper. Slater explained the System to Walker. The young

Tory had financial links in the City that Slater lacked. Like a couple of raiders mining the ramparts before an assault, the two combined talents and formed Slater, Walker Ltd. It was 1964. With an unintended irony, they were setting out to achieve by manipulation of the "market forces" and for their own ends what Harold Wilson was planning to do by state intervention: bust up the League of Gentlemen.

To Walker there was a political rationale, the updating of free enterprise, as well as the more venal pleasure; for Slater such philosophizing was irrelevant. Like most commercial banditry, the success of the Slater, Walker assault depended on the somnolence of their victims. When Slater spotted an undervalued asset, it meant that somebody who should have known better was ignorant of the value of what they were sitting on. So it was with the partnership's first coup.

They found a near-derelict clothing firm called, as luck would have it, H. Lotery. The share price was well below the nominal breakup asset value. With $1,750,000 of mostly borrowed money, they took over Lotery and turned it into the shell of Slater, Walker Ltd. In the process the company's hidden asset, a central London office building, was sold for nearly $5 million. With land and property values escalating, Slater, Walker set the pattern for a new sport: asset stripping. Companies with sluggish earnings were bought up and cut down to a viable size, and the stripped-off assets were sold at high profit. It was remarkably easy, once the trick was learned, and it showed how comatose were many of the boardrooms populated by the League of Gentlemen. While the directors were out on the grouse moors or golf courses, the gimlet eye of Slater cased the company records. Then the predators moved in.

By 1968, asset-stripping was too conspicuous, even notorious. The gentlemen, now wise to the game, called Slater a jackal. Walker was getting sensitive about his political image. Since 1966 he had been inside Edward Heath's cabal of planners for the new Conservatism, an apostle of business reform. He didn't want to be tarnished as a wrecker rather than a builder. By then both he and Slater were multimillionaires. They could afford to look for something more elegant.

And so the strippers became bankers. With more fancy footwork they bought a small bank, Ralli Brothers, and transformed it into an international investment network. With this under way, Slater, Walker took a symbolic step. They moved offices from the West End of London through the gates and into the City of London. They then began the complex process of selling off their industrial interests—more than $100 million worth—and spinning them off into partly owned satellites. From share speculations they moved to stripping, from stripping to industrial conglomerates, from that into banking. Each move had been ahead of the game or, as one Slater, Walker protégé put it: "It's a sort of mirror trick, trying to keep ahead of the dirty word."

By 1970 Slater and Walker were each reckoned to have made their first $20 million.

There is a way in Britain of defining a particular kind of lassitude when it goes with an effete nature. It is called "wet." There are wet people and wet behavior. In this sense the antonym of *wet* is not *dry,* but *mean.*

The absence of Teutonic dedication in British corporate managers is regarded as wet by men who would rather be mean. Wetness is not a failing of Peter Walker or of Jim Slater, or of Edward Heath.

As he watched the shambles of British business, Heath saw too much wetness and too many wets. Edward Heath is not a sympathetic man; he has an emetic laugh, he is so bad at small talk that he walks around at parties in his own portable limbo. There is a certain insouciance in his manner that can chill the most convivial company.

He is a bit of a Boy Scout and, in spite of his ample girth, an enemy of getting "soft." Wetness drives him crazy.

In 1970, with Heath's blessing, Peter Walker took his gun-slinging style into government. He had made himself rich beyond the dreams of a lower-class suburban boyhood, and far richer than Heath, who was from a similar background. But some of Walker's golden touch seems to have rubbed off on Heath. Between 1965 and 1968, when Slater, Walker took off, Heath did remarkably well with a modest investment of $21,000; just how well he didn't say. But if Slater could turn $5,000 into $125,000 in a year, Heath—with the right advice—wouldn't be badly off. He confirmed that he left the management of his money to others, and no doubt Walker obliged.

The outward evidence of Heath's escalating good fortune was three yachts: Morning Cloud I, bought for $17,500; replaced by Morning Cloud II, bought for $52,000 and sold for $87,000; and Morning Cloud III, bought in 1973 for $112,500. Getting wet the Heath way meant hard, rugged sailing. This was made clear a few months after he took the helm of the country:

> Our purpose is to bring our fellow citizens to recognize that they must be responsible for the consequences of their own actions and to learn that no one will stand between them and the results of their own free choice.

With Walker at his elbow, Heath decided that the country needed a rigorous course in the art of not being wet. Looking with a mean eye at British industry, a Heath minister warned, "The government will not help lame ducks across ponds or assist a morass of subsidized incompetence."

The League of Gentlemen couldn't believe what they were hearing: a *Tory* government abandoning the cosy compact of state and business, prepared to allow the weakest to go to the wall? And since the most vulnerable of the weak were the totems of True Brit, how could Heath be so hard of heart? They needn't have worried. Faced with the imminent collapse of Rolls-Royce, the most illustrious of those totems, Heath relented. Non-wet did not extend to allowing Rolls-Royce to wipe itself out. Similar somersaults followed. Heath was as prone to the hallucinations of True Brit as anyone.

If propping up the superannuated symbols of True Brit was *not* wet, what was? *The Times,* that erstwhile supporter of government by tycoon, had its own idea. In the course of a eulogy of Herr Willy Brandt, the West German chancellor, it said:

> As nationally we are going through a wet mood, we are lucky not to have a wet Prime Minister. . . . The German people, with their serious and authoritarian family life and educational system, are a well-disciplined people. The British educational system was never as highly disciplined, and what elements of discipline it used to have are for better or worse now much reduced. . . .

It was a long time since anyone had dared to suggest to the British that German "discipline" was an inspiration. Free copies of *Mein Kampf* available on request. . . . But *The Times* had two favorite images of British wetness: students and labor unions. Certainly nobody could describe the German treatment of either students or unions as forgiving. If only, mused the Teutons on *The Times,* we could be like that. . . .

While Slater, Walker and the City hustlers were screwing the gentlemen, whom had the gentlemen been screwing?

The sheep in the City of London are the small investors. In spite of the growth of mutual funds, the fleecing of the sheep got so bad that—against all the trends—the number of shareholders in Britain actually declined, at the rate of 5 percent a year. The contest between lay ignorance and professional smartness is too unequal. Small investors are the cannon fodder of the Hustlers. These investors rely on shares to subsidize meager pensions. They are inexpert in the new arts of the market; they have no way of reading signs and playing dirty tricks. Their interests are supposed to be in the care of the Stock Exchange Council. But, like all the instruments of the League of Gentlemen, the council is a case of the robbers policing the robbers. It is composed entirely of the self-sustaining clique of brokers and jobbers who put their own interests above the public's.

There is no watchdog with anything like the teeth of the Securities and Exchange Commission in the United States, as fallible as even that is. The surge of takeovers and mergers made insider dealing, outlawed in the United States, a lucrative game in the City of London. Anybody with an inside track—which means the professional analysts—would read the signs of an incipient bid and could make a killing if they were unscrupulous. Rich pickings were made by executives inside the companies involved.

This became so flagrant that the gentlemen set up a panel to monitor takeovers and mergers. Its methods were laughable. The ethics of the club were at work again. The panel's inquiries were conducted, said its director general, in an atmosphere of "polite exchanges." And, giving the whole game away, he added, "We probably catch the less intelligent, not the man who has set out to act dishonestly and has covered his tracks well."

An even truer glimpse of the tortured ethics of the City came from the chairman of the Stock Exchange, who allowed that insider dealing was "no better than stealing," but said that the public was outraged by it not because some people had made a pile, but because *it* hadn't.

"Keeping ahead of the dirty word," the two original Hustlers had the nerve themselves to complain about the legalized lawlessness in the City. Insider dealing, said Slater, was giving business a bad name. From his new position in Whitehall, Walker was also vocally disapproving. When Walker joined the Heath cabinet in 1970, he sold his Slater, Walker shares, but the company kept his name and the two moved in parallel. Although still not overtly political, Slater supported the Tories from company funds, at the rate of about $37,000 a year. Edward Heath, according to Slater, was "the personification of meritocracy in politics." Heath was certainly good for business, and business was good for Slater. But Slater and Walker went one stage further than that: what was good for business was good for Britain.

At the heart of non-wetness is a belief in the national virtue of making a fast buck. The Tories should, said Slater, "generate an atmosphere in which success and profit in business are regarded as important and in the interest of the country." Lord Stokes, still desperately saddled with his wayward auto giant, sang the same song. The endemic lack of ambition, the feigned diffidence toward money, the social snobbery against the Hustlers—these were the traits of wetness that Heath and the Hustlers abhorred. "I think," said Slater, "Slater, Walker played a part in the reformation of British industry, and to this extent we have certainly contributed to the country's welfare, as well as in the more direct material sense."

Turning his hand to an equally glib self-justification, Walker said, "Capitalism should not be regarded as the means for a few to get rich." And to an audience of assembled industrialists, he laid out the rules of non-wet management with the simple fervor of a Boy Scout:

> Be efficient and make a profit for Britain.
> Don't pollute.
> Look after the workers.
> Don't cheat.
> Uphold the national objectives.

And, he might have added, take a cold shower every morning.

Walker called this threadbare code the "New Capitalism." The Hustlers desperately wanted the British to regard making money as an *acceptable motivation.* But those who did have plenty of money didn't want to talk about it, and those who didn't weren't concerned with niceties like whether or not business was socially taboo; they would simply have liked to see some of the money coming their way.

Perhaps why the Hustlers craved so openly for a kind of ethical acceptance was that they still felt excluded from the club, even after their noble work in the reformation of derelict industry. They were right, as Slater discovered in the most galling way.

He had built a company with earnings of nearly $50 million a year, but he wanted something better. He dreamed of a new-style *banque d'affaires,* a kind of multinational financial empire, which British entry of the Common Market made logical.

Slater spent six weeks secretly negotiating with Sir Kenneth Keith, chairman of the merchant bank Hill, Samuel. Keith is a man of two parts. The bottom part has the stout thighs of a landowning squire; the top part, the rapier mind of a veteran manipulator. Keith had what Slater lacked: a subtlety of style. He had engineered many takeovers, but without attracting the displeasure of the club. He and his bank had the dignity Slater knew he needed.

With such a coup, Slater would become a primary power in the City. But there was more to it than that—an anointment that money could not buy. In the tightly cross-bred blood lines of the City of London, Slater was still an outsider. The social exclusivity of the old money is as durable as its monopoly of the financial institutions. Combing the membership lists of the nine most influential London clubs reveals the directors of these financial institutions spread throughout them; Hill, Samuel has directors belonging to three of the nine, Boodle's, Pratt's, and White's. Slater, Walker is nowhere. The *nouveau riche* need not apply.

To get the status that the merger promised, Slater was prepared to be humble. He accepted a deal in which the Slater, Walker name would disappear into a joint empire, and in which he would play second fiddle to Keith. It didn't seem like the old Slater style; some wondered whether he was losing his touch, even whether he was ill.

Ironically, it fell to Walker as the minister of Industry to decide whether the Slater–Hill, Samuel deal should be referred to the Monopolies Commission or allowed to go ahead. Aware of his embarrassment, Walker deputed the decision to a deputy who, not without taking flak, gave the green light. United, the Slater-Keith operation would have had gross assets of $3.75 billion, making it the equal in international capability of First National City Bank of New York. But it was not to be. As they got down to stitching the two outfits together, Slater and Keith discovered in each other serious divergencies of style. Slater was not a natural second man, and Keith was too dominant to move sideways.

When the deal was called off, there were audible sighs of relief from the League of Gentlemen. Slater was to them a cad, a bounder, an upstart, an outsider—not the kind of chap who ought to be allowed in the club, whatever the size of his bank balance. But the gentlemen were less pleased by Walker's next caper. Trickery in the City had become so bad, he said, that there would have to be new and much tougher company laws. Many people saw the cynicism of his own role reversal. And expert observers felt that creating laws did not automatically stop lawlessness. The artful dodges were too ingrained, too recondite, to be deterred by what was, after all, cosmetic politics.

Slater, meanwhile, did what many of his native fore-
bears had done when ostracized or persecuted in their
own country: he headed west. A hefty batch of American
companies was analyzed by the Slater, Walker computer,
according to the criteria of the System. A short list of ten
became targets for takeover. From the bridgehead of the
Franklin Stores Corp., which he acquired for its New
York Stock Exchange listing, Slater showed his old rapacious spirit, sublimated in London but tempted again in
Manhattan. "We would prefer a friendly merger, but if a
deal seems reasonably attractive now we will fight for it,"
he told a Dow Jones reporter. But within six months of
that cocky statement, Slater pulled out of New York, having lost more than $5 million. He had overreached him-
self, and was badly burned.

The Slater, Walker raids have meaning as a paradigm of the political effort to smash the hold and expose
the methods of the gentlemen. Slater and Walker en-
riched themselves rather than the country, but at the
start their freebooting piracy was more disruptive to the
old order than the government policies which, instead of
spilling blood in the City, built the axis between finance
and industry on one side and a gullible but omnipotent
bureaucracy on the other. In the end, though, the two
pirates—like so many other erstwhile challengers of the
British system—were prepared to stand on their heads to
be accepted by that system.

Walker grabbed to the full Heath's invitation to bring
non-wet dealing into government, but he had to try to
make it palatable with the disingenuous gloss of the
"New Capitalism." Slater, a much more private person,
rode thoughtfully in the back of his Bentley calculating
the steps to his metamorphosis as an international
banker, rewriting his own history as he went. Both are
like a couple of small boys who have been caught poach-
ing on the estate and then marry into the owner's family.
They can drink a Sunday-morning sherry with the hunt,

but they can never, however much they crave it, be accepted as one of Them.

The ruling elite of the City survives without dilution. It is drawn from a remarkably narrow and sharply defined stratum, beginning with kinships, nurtured through public schools, with Eton the most dominant, refined by Oxbridge, and cemented by the dual intercourse of the executive suite and the exclusive clubs. The same families stay on top, and the financial decisions, crucial to most of British business, taken by the banks, insurance companies, and other institutions are, in the end, in the gift of a few men of identical background and outlook. It was gauche of Slater to try to break such a conspiracy.

Jimmy Goldsmith runs a European conglomerate from London and Paris under a main company called Générale Occidentale. Goldsmith and his operations are often held up as an example of what success in business should really be, and he himself agrees. British business, he says, "needed a major shakeup, because it seemed that our industrial caste system was beginning to fail." Goldsmith admires Jim Slater and his spirit.

Early in 1973 he gave a coming-out party for his daughter at the Ritz Hotel in London. There were 250 guests. The London *Evening Standard* reported:

> The basement bar was transformed into a semitropical garden with a strong Louisiana theme: five Negro orchestras were flown in from New Orleans. Ten members of the bands had never left New Orleans before. Two were blind and had "gammy" legs. One of the most spectacular of the bands came prancing on the scene wearing enormous red and white Red Indian headgear and feathers.
>
> There was not a plastic plant in the entire place and orchids overflowed everywhere. The floor was carpeted with chopped-up wine corks. The guests were a remarkable cross-section of Bohemian society, big business and Continental high society. . . .

The dinner was a full-scale affair with Creole specialities. A cold buffet was kept running throughout the night, consisting mainly of game. The wines were Bollinger NV and Château Palmer 1964 in magnums.

The party was still going strong up to five this morning with the New Orleans bands alternating and rivalling each other in what was a positive festival of brilliant jazz. . . .

Before Edward Heath, no Conservative prime minister, whatever the provocation, had the nerve to bite the hand that fed the party funds. Attacks on capitalism are normally left to the Labour party, and even they can be ambivalent about it. So that when, in the House of Commons, Heath described one company as "the unpleasant and unacceptable face of capitalism," it was a historic as well as a rhetorical moment. As the man who had legitimized the Hustlers, Heath needed to be careful about finding targets for his abuse. In this case, he could hardly have kept silent.

As the British pulled out of Africa in the 1950s and '60s, they left unstable political situations and nascent economies. For anyone with an eye for business opportunities it was a risky but potentially lucrative field of operation. British businessmen, used for so long to having captive and monopolized markets, could no longer rely on their imperial airs and graces—nor were they popular. But the emergent countries badly needed technical expertise and men who could build up their trade. Roland ("Tiny") Rowland, well over six feet tall, was a man who saw this chance and who happened to be equipped for it.

Rowland was born in India, the son of a German trader. Because of this parentage he was put into detention in Britain during World War II. After the war he drifted from one fruitless job to another, and then emigrated to Rhodesia. In the calm of the colonial twilight he prospered as a farmer. In England the sallow skin of the Anglo-Indian had marked him out; in Rhodesia, among the tanned white settlers, Rowland developed British upper-class manners and accent in an almost exaggerated self-grooming. He became a surrogate gentleman. But there was just enough of the exotic about him, and an indomitable charm, to avoid the harder, patrician edge that Africans disliked in the style of the whites. Without quite realizing it, Rowland had acquired the ideal characteristics for an entrepreneur in the new Africa.

Sometime in 1960, Rowland met a young British businessman in Rhodesia, a man of impeccable connections and a rising reputation as a shrewd dealer. The Honorable Angus Ogilvy was a director of a banking group that had invested in a company called the London and Rhodesian Mining Company, or Lonrho for short. Ogilvy was not happy with the way Lonrho was going, and he decided after meeting Rowland that this beguiling man had just the kind of energy the company needed. In 1961 Ogilvy put Lonrho into Rowland's care. It was a happy inspiration, and a rapport grew rapidly between the two men. When Rowland joined Lonrho, its net profits before tax were $394,000. By 1972 they were $48.2 million. In that time Rowland had acquired four hundred subsidiary companies. Lonrho's interests were spun intricately through both black and white Africa, including railways, mining, auto dealerships, and newspapers. In three of the new African states, Zambia, Zaïre, and Ghana, the political leaders regarded Rowland as almost a national asset.

The fact that Rowland's intimate colleague on the Lonrho board was Angus Ogilvy, husband of Princess Alexandra, a cousin of the queen, did not hurt. The princess had helped out the royal family in the arduous chore of attending the ceremonials when for the last time the Union Jack was lowered in colonial outposts. She is paid $25,000 a year for her public services.

Although on its record Lonrho seemed a model testimony to Rowland's talents, there were growing problems in its accounts. It was a London-based company, quoted on the London Stock Exchange, but most of its earnings came from Africa, and much of its profits were unremittable to London. At the end of 1971 the money flowing out from London to finance new projects had outstripped the money coming in, and there was a cash crisis. Ogilvy commissioned a report into Lonrho's finances by accountants. This uncovered the consequences of Rowland's highly personal style of running the company. He had built the business on his own contacts—without Rowland there would have been no Lonrho. But Rowland had little patience with bureaucratic procedure or the boardroom consensus. He blew by the seat of his pants, and he preferred to fly solo. This style was anathema to the conventional corporate accountants, and it cut corners on the codes of business practice, such as they were.

Although Ogilvy wanted a semblance of orthodoxy imposed on Lonrho, he knew better than anybody that Rowland carried the company. He was not anxious to see Rowland's wings clipped. His solution was window dressing. Lonrho would acquire some gentlemen.

It was a noble intention, but management by gray eminence was inimical to Rowland's temperament. And one of the new Lonrho directors seemed to have been picked to represent the antithesis of everything that Rowland was. Sir Basil Smallpeice represented a kind of instant sobriety. He was highly esteemed by the City Establishment on grounds that seemed almost wholly negative: his personality had been sublimated by prudence. His arid pedantry had served him well as managing director of BOAC, an airline run like a branch of the civil service. His later chairmanship of the shipping line Cunard had ended when that company's conservative accounting made it a prime target for rape by takeover. The Hustlers moved in and Smallpeice moved out. He was stripped along with the assets.

When Smallpeice took over as deputy chairman of

Lonrho and began to get a sense of Rowland's cavalier style, his demeanor, which normally suggested a man walking in fear of offensive odors, became acutely discomfited. Recoiling from an excursion into the company accounts, Smallpeice consulted other directors and emerged as the leader of a dissenting caucus. As the board became polarized between Rowland and the Smallpeice faction, another distinctly singular character popped up in the middle. Rowland had made his own move to recruit a figure of esteem, somebody who could both ingratiate Lonrho back into the City's favors and at the same time lubricate its African business. His choice was the Right Honorable Duncan Sandys, M.P.

The appearance of Sandys in the story, which was to become crucial, requires a digression toward more illustrious adventures than the construction of an African business empire. Sandys represents a strange breed in British political life, as the survivor of a once-elite band whose fortunes and reputation revealed the country's internal convulsions and external bravura.

One of Sandys's colleagues in a postwar Tory cabinet called him one of those "overgrown Boy Scouts." This was a bit harsh. Sandys had behind him one of the most valuable and least acknowledged coups of World War II, the crippling of Wernher Von Braun's V-2 rocket sites, which, according to Eisenhower, made the D-Day landings possible. When Sandys, in RAF intelligence, detected the sites, the top military brass reacted with scorn and disbelief. But Sandys had leverage. He was Churchill's son-in-law. The RAF was ordered to blast the launching pads.

Not only marriage tied Sandys to the Churchill clan. Before the war he had been an opponent of appeasement; after the war he encouraged Churchill into a theme of European unity. But on the way he contracted a fatal flaw: hyperpatriotism that curdled easily into imperial lament. At Suez Sandys was a gunboat diplomatist. As the colonies were shed, he rushed around Africa trying to ensure that the new nations were respectful of British values. He lectured their leaders in the best Old Etonian manner. He loved telling the story of how he found President Kwame Nkrumah of Ghana cowering from public view because he feared assassination. Sandys insisted Nkrumah take a ride through Accra in an open car and, for good measure, forced him out of the car and into the crowds. As Sandys described it, the moral was that the British spirit could put back the spine into the most abject coward. When the colonies came to Britain, Sandys was an early hard-liner against immigration.

With this kind of history, it might have seemed tactless of Rowland to recruit Sandys to the cause of maintaining Lonrho's good relations in black Africa, but Sandys was so thick-skinned that any suggestion of white paternalism amazed him. Moreover, he was politically versatile enough to have kept useful contacts in South Africa.

Without consulting the board, Rowland hired Sandys as a consultant at $125,000 a year. Three months later, this was increased by $2,500 and the contract extended to six years. All but $4,500 of this money was to be paid into a tax haven in the Cayman Islands as an "overseas fee." But Rowland decided that he needed Sandys in a more visible role. The consultancy deal was scrapped and Sandys was appointed chairman at $100,000 a year. This apparent sacrifice was more than compensated for. Rowland paid Sandys $325,000 into the Cayman Islands as settlement for the loss of a consultancy that the Lonrho board didn't even know about until two weeks after they formally invited him to be chairman.

All this made Smallpeice apopleptic, but, for a while, Rowland had the continuing support of Ogilvy, his original sponsor. Sandys, naturally, backed Rowland, and so did another newly recruited piece of financial ballast, Edward du Cann. Whereas Sandys represented the amputated Churchillian limb of the Conservative party, du

Cann was a founding member of the Hustler's academy of the new capitalism. He was a former colleague of Peter Walker, and a former chairman of the Conservative party. He arrived at Lonrho as chairman of the merchant bank Keyser, Ullmann.

For a company with problems, Lonrho had attracted heavyweight support. This face of capitalism was well connected—with the Tories, with the City, with the lingering aura of Churchill and, by reflected glory, with the royal family. (As well as the Ogilvy connection, Smallpeice had once served as comptroller at Buckingham Palace, charged with the task of introducing modern business methods to the household management, without conspicuous success.)

It is axiomatic in the City Establishment's code that if shit is about to hit the fan, the room should empty quickly before the innocent are contaminated. As the Smallpeice faction became rebellious, the Honorable Angus Ogilvy regretfully resigned from the board of Lonrho "because of the situation that has arisen." Lonrho's dirty linen was about to be not just washed in public but flaunted.

Smallpeice, who would rather have lost his pants than his probity, led eight Lonrho directors who wanted Rowland sacked. To stop them, Rowland applied for an injunction in the High Court. This meant that for several days an incredulous nation was treated to a recital of charge and countercharge disclosing intrigue, high living, and rapacity and accompanied by the sound of collapsing reputations. Nothing quite like it had ever come from the mouths of gentlemen in public.

An important part of Smallpeice's case concerned complex and opaque dealings in Africa, some involving the Ogilvy family trusts. But it was not these that caught the public attention. Rowland's grand style of living, including a $977,000 country mansion donated free by the company, triggered a wail of puritan horror. So, too, did the details of Rowland's open-handed treatment of Sandys, especially the use of the tax haven.

Although Sandys immediately declared that $110,000 handed over as the first installment of his "compensation," destined for the Cayman Islands, had been paid back to Lonrho, these dealings made Sandys, as much as Rowland, a target for public outrage. Sandys's response, totally in character, was to clench his simian jaw even more tightly and say that the attacks on Rowland "were mostly of a very vague nature." Rowland had good cause to reflect that if (in the words of Montgomery about Mao Tse-tung) you wanted a man to go into the jungle with you, Duncan Sandys was a good choice.

The High Court ruled in favor of Smallpeice, but had to yield the final constitutional sanction to the Lonrho shareholders. "Whichever way the voting goes," said the chairman of a body called the Wider Share Ownership Council, "this is shareholder democracy in action." The shareholders voted six to one to keep Rowland and dump Smallpeice and his supporters.

On the face of it, the cavalier had been vindicated against the puritan. The sentiment of the shareholders —at least, the hundreds of them who turned up for the public vote—was clearly that Rowland was a man who made empires and that Smallpeice was a man who filled ledgers. (Rowland complained that during his tenure at Lonrho Smallpeice never once visited any of the African operations.) The assembled shareholders seemed predominantly *petit-bourgeois,* from the massed ranks of the Tory grass roots. They were unimpressed by appeals that tax havens and company mansions were immoral. They probably sensed, correctly, the cant in such a charge. The British shires are dotted with houses, cars, farms, racing stables, and boats that are funded by companies. Gentlemen regarded these as the legitimate fruits of capitalism. As for screwing the tax man, well, everybody was in favor of that. One shareholder explained,

"Tiny is a latter-day saint of capitalism, the sort of man to whom the small shareholder will entrust his life savings." Exit Smallpeice, seeking other employment.

Not only Sandys, du Cann, and the shareholders had backed Rowland; several of the black African leaders intimated that if he were to disappear, they would take a very poor view of it. They certainly didn't share Harold Wilson's predictable description of Lonrho as "a fetid swamp in the Tory free-for-all jungle."

For Heath the Lonrho affair had been uncomfortable. His definition of it as the "unpleasant and unacceptable face of capitalism" had been impulsive, but it reflected a revulsion that was apolitical. The roles of Sandys and du Cann stung him personally. Du Cann was chairman of a powerful pressure group of Tory M.P.'s, and he made a point of being evangelistic about his work in establishing, with Walker, British mutual funds. It was all uncomfortably close to the "new capitalism"; only Rowland's flamboyancy marked it out from the more bloodless calculations of the Slater, Walker history.

It is understandable that Heath should have been ambivalent about big business. On the one hand, he was its most committed supporter; on the other, he was continually provoked into anger by dilatory managements that put self-interest before the national interest. Heath was like a man doing social work among the whores in the hope of redeeming them; each time one of them dropped her skirts in public the embarrassment was acute. The Lonrho affair was a microcosm of all the social, political, and commercial attitudes dogging the path of reformers. As such, it seemed a good deal more real than any of the pious appeals to the public spirit.

9. OIL FROM TROUBLED WATERS

A Case History in Management by Custodian

The axis created in Whitehall between industry and government put major industrial policy into the hands of the Custodians. Ostensibly the decision-makers were supposed to be politicians. Actually, the complexity of the issues and the uncertain tenancy of governments meant that the interpretation of any situation provided by the bureaucrats predetermined the political decision. Since this interpretation was being provided by men who were themselves out of their depth, in a commercial atmosphere they found distasteful, the process was not only undemocratic but highly accident-prone.

The North Sea oil bonanza is definitive as a case history of Great Britain Ltd. in action. In six years the management of the oil exploration ran through three separate ministries, each representing a phase in the fumbling escalation of the central bureaucracies.

The North Sea is an inverted wedge of water, at its widest between Norway and the outer Scottish islands, and ending in a narrow thirty-mile-wide spout between England and northern France. Its depth at the northern end is over four hundred feet; at the southern end it is half that. The North Sea forms a funnel for winds and storms: it is one of the most treacherous stretches of water in the world. It is relatively shallow because it is a part of the European continental shelf; that shelf is traversed by basins, platforms, and trenches. There are similar basins in Russia, North Africa, Australia, west Texas, Oklahoma, and western Canada. Wherever they occur, these basins have one thing in common. There is a high chance that they will bear oil in commercial quantities.

Offshore rigs in the Gulf of Texas and the Caribbean are to the North Sea what the Ritz in Paris is to a fur trapper's cabin. Even when geologists began to look at the North Sea seriously as a possible oil field, in the 1950s, the idea of anyone getting a rig out into that mendacious water and staying alive long enough to sink a bore hole seemed a little unhinged. But oil prospectors these days are not so easily discouraged. The world's supplies are running out; Britain had no fields of her own, and most of her supplies came from the politically precarious zones of Africa and the Middle East.

In 1958 Britain and other countries bordering the North Sea signed a convention apportioning shares of the continental shelf, carving up on the maps what they all hoped would prove to be an undersea gusher. And since Britain covers the whole western perimeter of the North Sea, hers was the lion's share, west of a line bisecting the sea from north to south. There was no guarantee either that oil was there or, if it was, that it would be worth drilling for, so that sheer acreage was not in itself a key to riches. The Netherlands, with a small slice of the deal, hit a rich gas field.

In 1964 British policy for exploring the North Sea for gas and oil was drawn up in Whitehall. By then, the world's major oil companies had warmed toward the North Sea. But in Whitehall nobody had any experience of oil prospecting. The British share of the oil business was relatively modest: there was British Petroleum, 48 percent owned by the British government, and Royal Dutch–Shell, an Anglo-Dutch company in which the British stake was 40 percent. The international oil business was dominated by the Americans.

So far as there was anything clear about British policy, it was that the country ought to do as well out of the exploitation of her own resources as she knew how. To put it simply, could the British be as smart as the Arabs? More than that: could they be as smart as the British oilmen who were used to dealing with Arabs? The negotiating skills acquired via an English upper-class education followed by years coping with the cunning of the Casbah were formidable. As they savored the prospects of the North Sea, against whom did the oilmen have to pitch their wits? Those civilized amateurs, the Custodians.

When negotiations opened, the Petroleum Division of the Ministry of Power had three administrators, no technical staff, two junior-grade "executive"-rank civil servants, and three clerks. When the oilmen walked in, it was a meeting of experience and innocence, of savvy and naïveté. The prize was an energy source worth billions. From the start the battle was unequal.

Instead of dealing like men sitting on a fortune, the Custodians behaved like mendicants. They were made to believe that they had to *persuade* the oilmen to start prospecting. The oilmen made a melodrama out of the problems of the North Sea. They said that exploration would be dangerous and costly and that the technology was unproven. There was enough truth in this to make it stick, but at that point the oilmen had all the marbles. The ministry had no staff geologists or any other relevant technical knowledge.

The terms the oilmen won were anything but onerous. There was a royalty rate of 12½ percent; a down payment of $15,625 per block of one hundred square miles covering six years, followed by an annual payment of $25,000 per block, rising to a maximum of $145,000. Within that time scale the highest rate applied only well into the life of a proven strike; barren blocks could be surrendered within the six-year period. A fruitful block could be held on those terms for forty-six years—there was no break clause, no scope for renegotiation.

The oil companies' psychological warfare was masterly. As well as making the ministry feel grateful that they were ready to take up the burden, they played another card, abetted by the Arabists in the Foreign Office. If the British terms were too stiff, they suggested, the Arabs would take the hint and follow suit. This deeply impressed the civil servants, who were very anxious not to instruct Arabs how to impoverish oil companies.

At first, the reputation of the North Sea seemed to be borne out. Three drilling rigs were lost. Thirteen men were drowned. A new kind of rig had to be designed. In December, 1965, a British Petroleum drill hit gas at a site thirty-five miles off the coast of Yorkshire. Between then and the end of 1967, three other major gas fields were found a little to the south. These gas strikes transformed British energy prospects. Ninety percent of British gas now comes from the North Sea; since 1967 the country's consumption of gas has more than doubled. But gas was, after all, only the hors d'oeuvre. Finding it indicated that the chances of hitting oil were good, and that was why the oilmen were there in the first place.

In 1969 Phillips Petroleum hit oil inside the Norwegian sector of the North Sea, under 230 feet of water in a field called Ekofisk. Although the Ekofisk strike confounded oil-company pessimism about viable oil fields, the Custodians were becoming alarmed that—after three rounds of license negotiations—interest in the North Sea seemed to be falling off. By 1969 the Petroleum Division in Whitehall had grown modestly to a total of twenty-one, including three technicians. Nothing had been done about providing independent geological information until 1967. The Custodians had been content to rely on what the oil companies told them. And as the scent of strikes grew stronger in the nostrils of the oilmen, the more they increased their skepticism in public.

With the coming of the Heath government in 1970, the Petroleum Division for the first time came under the eye of a professional oilman. The timing was crucial, because the civil servants were thoroughly taken in by the gloomy prognoses of the companies. In a Whitehall reorganization, the division was included in the new Department of Trade and Industry, whose minister was John Davies, a former managing director of Shell. But Davies failed to grasp how guillible his senior officials were being in negotiating with the oil companies. The ministry's policy was in the hands of Sir Robert Marshall, and during the six years of the Labour government they had resisted all attempts to stiffen the terms of the contracts, although there were already suspicions that a fortune was virtually being given away.

In 1970, as Davies took over, Marshall and his staff had been mousetrapped. Their case for generous contracts was that they wanted the resources tapped rapidly. But, even though the Ekofisk strike indicated rich oil sources, the civil servants had been panicked into believing that the companies were losing interest. All three previous rounds of oil licenses were what the ministry called "discretionary." Companies or consortia had to satisfy the ministry of their suitability and, on the original 1964 terms, they got the blocks. Nobody had proposed following the American practice of competitive auctions. Instead of parting with licenses for peanuts, this would have set a realistic market price for blocks of the North Sea.

But by 1971 the panic in the ministry was so acute that it decided to release 436 blocks for tender, including most of the promising fields. Almost as an afterthought, fifteen of the blocks were put up for auction as an experiment; the rest went on the 1964 terms. The auctioned blocks were mixed to include five reckoned to be poor, five moderate, and five promising. Experience had shown that "poor" blocks could yield strikes and "good" blocks turn out to be barren.

What then happened ought to have been the terminal indictment of nine years of peanut vending. Of the 436 blocks offered, 267 were taken up on the discretionary basis and produced for the ministry $7.5 million. The fifteen auctioned blocks produced $91 million. On a straight extrapolation of the market price established by the auction, all the blocks would have been worth $1,875 million instead of the $98.5 million raised. Even allowing that there was simply not that much money around for oil exploration, and that some blocks were more attractive than others, two things were painfully clear—the best part of the oil and gas fields had been as good as given away, and in the panic far more blocks had been allowed to go than should have been.

It was a gigantic and costly miscalculation. But Sir Robert Marshall and his staff were oblivious: they went ahead and compounded the fiasco. The discretionary contracts were allowed to go ahead, although by the time the auction result was in, no commitments had been made other than the advertised invitations. To then have revised the terms would have been, in Sir Robert's words, "a breach of faith." This was the language of a man playing a game of bridge in a Pall Mall club, rather than of a man just caught as the victim of a confidence trick.

Had Davies grasped what was going on? All the ministers who had been, from 1964, nominally responsible for North Sea oil policy had been swept along by their Custodians, either overtrusting or negligent. Asked later if he had told Davies about the implications of the auction, Sir Robert was evasive. "The minister was informed at once of the results of the auction. He knew that action was proceeding on the applications of the discretionary system. *He was not specifically reminded of the receipts from initial payments.*"

Thus the nimble side step from responsibility. On what terms would such a conversation take place? Did either man look the other in the eye?

This was not the whole extent of the ministry's miscalculations. It made three other expensive mistakes. By far the most costly, and most curious, had been to write into all its calculations of oil-company income an assumption that the profits made from the North Sea would carry the regular United Kingdom tax of more than 50 percent. This overlooked the fact that any oil company registered in the United Kingdom could charge as a "tax loss" against its profits all the royalties paid to other oil sources, mainly the Arabs. Since until then there had been no prospect of profits arising from U.K. wells, these "tax losses" had accumulated and were able to do so from year to year. And since the volume of oil on which royalties were paid elsewhere was far greater than the potential of the North Sea wells, and since the Arabs were raising their royalties, the "tax losses" would be so vast as to more than cover future profits from the North Sea.

In fact, by 1971 the companies had accumulated $4.5 billion in "tax losses," running by then at an average of $875 million a year. With the worth of North Sea oil at its peak in 1980 estimated at $5 billion a year, the companies were due for a "tax holiday" for years. They also got from the British government huge capital-development and depreciation allowances to further soften the burden.

As early as 1964, when the fatal policy was being

drawn up, the Internal Revenue Department had warned the Petroleum Division: "In discussions the companies and we have *tacitly accepted the fiction* that all companies will pay U.K. tax at the full rate. In fact we know that the two largest British companies pay hardly any tax in this country at the present time because of double taxation and other reliefs." This memorandum was conveniently buried and the "fiction" presented to ministers as a token of the suffering to be endured by the noble oil companies as they hit oil.

The two other errors helped to convey a picture of Britain getting an equitable piece of the action. The ministry had said that, through British holdings in the oil companies, the direct benefit to the country was 21 percent of the ownership of licensed territory. But this made the elementary mistake of assuming that Shell was a wholly British company; allowing for the fact that Britain had only 40 percent meant that the national stake was not 21 percent but 12 percent. The same sloppy work produced "evidence" that the British share of back-up services like pipelines and rigs was 50 percent, again on an assumption that companies operating in Britain were British. In many cases large slices of the profits were remitted elsewhere, mostly to the United States. The real British share was 25 percent.

But Sir Robert Marshall was unrepentant. The true face of the Custodian never lost its composure. After all the "fictions" and miscalculations were apparent, Sir Robert could only say, "In one way or another the market would have supported some strengthening of the terms and we may have made a misjudgment there, but I do not think it was a very large misjudgment."

In the auction, a consortium of Shell and Exxon had paid $50 million for one block. And they had not been flying by the seat of their pants.

After the years of negligence, Heath's government did the only thing it could do. It undertook to tax the

North Sea profits at the full rate. Davies was, with seeming decorum, moved from the trade ministry to become minister to Europe.

Had the oilmen been weeping crocodile tears? The perils of the North Sea were not exaggerated, but once the equipment was right, the score of successful oil strikes was extraordinarily high: one wildcat in every twelve yielded a viable supply; in the United States only one in fifty proves profitable. Even at a cost of between $2.5 and $5 million for opening a well, the North Sea is regarded as pay dirt. But perhaps the final giveaway comes from Sir Frank McFadzean, chairman of Shell in London. He admitted, "Every calculation we have made on investing has been on the basis that we would pay corporate tax on every barrel we take from the North Sea. We have always anticipated that the government would do what it is going to do."

In other words, the innocence of the Custodians had been too obvious to last. While it had, the oilmen took full advantage of it. They had never, for example, been asked or obliged to tell the ministry what their real costs were.

Through 1973 the rate of oil strikes in the northern sector of the British North Sea made the early pessimism evaporate. The bulk of the notorious fourth-round blocks were on the extreme northeastern perimeter, including the highest-priced one of all, block 211/21 bought by Shell/Exxon, which was between the Shetland Islands and Norway. For the languishing economy of Scotland, the oil rush was a new Klondike. For Britain, the strikes held out the prospects of meeting two-thirds, 150 million tons, of the country's oil needs by 1980. The first wells came on stream in 1974, lessening the vulnerable dependence on Mediterranean supplies.

In 1973 the Petroleum Division of the Department of Trade and Industry, its gifts dispensed, announced an increase in its staff of experts, from ten to twenty.

10. DREAMING THE IMPOSSIBLE DREAM

The Overselling of True Brit

If the British were selling True Brit only to themselves it would be bad enough, but they are out there selling it to other people. They have to: it's export or perish. The point of creating the corporate state was to gear up lagging industry to compete in the international markets. But a lot of that effort has come to naught. True Brit has overreached.

Surrender of the empire was a *fait accompli*. But the state of mind behind it did not disappear; it lives on as a commercial and technical fantasy. The really big disasters in the selling of True Brit—and they are epic—are all traceable to this delusion. The country cannot match its efforts to its resources because, in doing so, it would have to admit the unthinkable: it is no longer the champ.

In 1945 Britain, despite being drained by war, was ahead of America in computers, jet engines, and radar and saw much sooner the potential of nuclear energy for domestic use. In all of these she has long since been outdistanced by the United States and other countries. One of the few remaining ideas to support the notion of British inventive primacy, the linear induction motor, has been sabotaged by government ineptitude. Technology in Britain has been made ridiculous not only by bad management but by the heroic demands made of it in the name of British legend.

It was the old Desert Fox himself, Field Marshal Erwin Rommel, who noticed his adversary's failing. It was, he said, part of the British character to produce good ideas and then fail to exploit them. Rommel was smart enough to steal the theory of tank warfare from the British and to use it devastatingly against them. The British might have taken the tip and specialized in selling ideas to people more able to do justice to them. Instead, in the frenzy of True Brit, they have tried to be both innovator and seller, with lamentable results. It does, as Rommel suspected, seem to be a flaw of character.

THE IMPOSSIBLE DREAM (1): ROLLS-ROYCE GOES BANANAS

Three seemingly enduring symbols of True Brit were once the Bank of England, the Rock of Gibraltar, and Rolls-Royce. In any all-purpose kit of patriotic totems, these had no equal. The Bank stood for the sanctity of the pound sterling, the rock for imperial impregnability, and Rolls-Royce for things that worked and went on working. All three have fallen. But the collapse of Rolls-Royce was the hardest for the British to take.

When David Ogilvy renewed the Rolls legend in America in the 1950s with the slogan "At 60 mph the only sound you'll hear is the ticking of the clock," he had what every adman dreams of: a product seemingly so good that it hardly needed selling. The Rolls had something more than superlative craftsmanship and engineering excellence. It had mystique.

But the car division was an increasingly minor part of the Rolls business. The company's fortunes depended on aero engines. Rolls were the first to make the jet engine a reliable proposition. For two decades its jets were unsurpassed. But there came a point, for Rolls and for Britain, where going one jump further in technology came perilously close to getting out of their depth—financially and technically. It was the crunch of matching ambition to resources. Going beyond that point involved Rolls in doing something wholly against its character. It had to be reckless.

Rolls alone can't be blamed for this. It was pulled along in the collective hallucination. The pride of Britain was at stake.

The cause of Rolls's downfall was its deal in 1968 with Lockheed to produce the RB 211 engine for the Tristar. To the British it meant breaking into the American domestic market and cocking a snoot at their toughest opposition. When the deal was signed, the reaction was like a national virility rite. Even normally sane newspapers went into a chauvinistic delirium. "BRITAIN IS BETTER THAN ANYONE ELSE IN THE WORLD," said *The Observer*. And the Duke of Edinburgh, a tireless optimist, wired the firm: "Delighted you have pulled off the deal."

Two years later the British prime minister called up President Nixon in Washington on the hot line. There is no public record of the conversation. But it's worth imagining that it went something like this:

EDWARD HEATH: Er, I say, Mr. President, I have some rather bad news. Rolls-Royce is going bankrupt.
RICHARD NIXON: Who?
HEATH: Rolls-Royce . . . you know, *the* Rolls-Royce.

NIXON: Too bad. What should I do about it, Prime Minister?

HEATH: Well, Mr. President, it looks as if Lockheed are going to have a new plane without any engines.

NIXON: Is that right? Could you make that perfectly clear?

HEATH: We've put about two hundred million dollars into Rolls and the engine still won't come right. I can't see how we alone can do anything more. But perhaps if Lockheed means anything to you . . .

NIXON: You're damn right it does. It's a California company.

HEATH: I thought you might get the point.

NIXON: See here, Prime Minister, I can't guarantee you anything, but I'll have you transferred to the Department of Defense.

HEATH: The Department of *Defense?*

NIXON: I have a man in there called Packard. He'll help you all he can. He has access to funds. With an election coming up, we can't have an airplane in California without any engines. But I wish you guys would wise up and get out of the aerospace business. . . .

Packard and Heath talked, and in the austere language of the official record, "no undertakings were given on either side and the two governments agreed to keep in touch." It was a frosty moment in Anglo-American diplomacy. The British felt they had been mousetrapped by the Lockheed deal, the Americans felt that Rolls-Royce had been spectacularly inept in its calculations. But Lockheed had to be kept in the air for much the same reasons that Rolls-Royce had to be saved: the political blowback of failure was a more acute pressure than sheer cost.

Although the official British inquiry tried to palm off the blame on the Rolls executives, the real guilt was as much in Whitehall as in the Rolls works at Derby. The civil servants overseeing the production of the RB 211 included, as it happened, Sir Robert Marshall, who had been so generous in dispensing the North Sea oil licenses. There were two peculiarities about the contract between Rolls and Lockheed: nobody in Whitehall had even seen it until months after it was signed, and British government aid had never before been advanced for a project governed by a contract signed in the American courts. The aberration of Rolls throwing caution to the winds was rather like an English village parson getting smashed and riding his bicycle recklessly. So much did the company covet the Lockheed deal that it fixed a price for each engine without allowing for either inflation or technical problems—and it accepted punitive penalty clauses if it failed to meet performance goals and delivery dates. Yet when the contract was signed, the RB 211 was little more than a gleam in its designers' eyes, an engine that, in order to work, had to prove a number of unproven concepts. Immaculate conception is not a common feature of the aerospace business, not even at Rolls-Royce.

In reality, the Rolls people had gone bananas. They were locked into a contract they couldn't meet. They had been wildly overoptimistic on the development program. They had even cooked their accounts, writing down an inventory as assets to conceal a serious cash shortage. Lockheed, with troubles of its own, could be merciless with such a contract, and was.

Under this pressure something happened that must have made Sir Henry Royce, the engineering genius, spin in his grave. Rolls cut corners. A first batch of RB 211 engines had been bug-ridden, but promising. A second batch, rushed through to try to meet the Lockheed deadline, was disastrous. The fine engineering tolerances necessary had not been met. Performance was so bad, with hot gases leaking, that the engines had to be rebuilt. It was mortifying for the self-respect of the Rolls engineers, and mortal for the company.

A powerful *Zeitgeist* inhabited Rolls, the spirit of genius at the workshop bench. For years the engineers feared that the company's original spark could easily be snuffed out if corporate organization superseded the worth of individuals. Even when a $30 million IBM computer bank was installed, the tradition of the maverick engineer was allowed to persist. The RB 211 dénouement was more than the unraveling of a mystique—it was the end of the road for "seat-of-the-pants" judgment in a business that had thrived on it.

The RB 211 had sucked in money and burned it in much the same way that it was supposed to suck in air, with the same impunity. Its final cost was $500 million, most of it public money. Sir Robert Marshall, bruised but still a model of civil-service sangfroid, admitted that at the time the ministry was funding the project it regarded Rolls to be as safe as the Bank of England. It was an unhappy comparison, as well as a revealing remark. Rescuing Rolls buried Edward Heath's declared commitment to non-wetness. There were plaintive statements about "our reputation as a trading nation and as leaders in technology" and about Rolls-Royce's "high technical reputation." A more believable epitaph was spoken by Sir Robert Marshall:

> It would be quite silly for anybody with knowledge of these things to suppose that mishaps on a considerable scale could not occur again.

He should know. He was also involved in another flight of the British spirit that makes Rolls-Royce look like a minor plumbing error.

THE IMPOSSIBLE DREAM (2): UP, UP, AND AWAY IN THE GREAT WHITE BIRD

It has it all: rampant True Brit, anti-Americanism, Anglo-French chauvinism, technical overreach, executive concealment, the massive diversion of public funds into the accounts of delinquent corporations, contempt for the environment, the pursuit of narrow political self-interest, and the gross distortion of social priorities. The

Concorde, the Anglo-French supersonic airliner, eclipses any other misadventure in the pursuit of national glory. In more rational times it would be seen as the definitive scandal of its kind, the chilling proof that technology can subvert sanity and the democratic processes.

The Concorde covers a decade and a half of European history. This life-span is the key to its survival. It shows how such a project can outlive its creators—governments, departments, and dreamers. When some of its begetters realized their error, the Thing had taken on a life of its own. It could not be stopped.

Its origins are political. The Concorde grew directly from the mentality that plotted the 1956 invasion of Suez, the most conspicuous postwar example of Anglo-French collusion. Only six years separated Suez and the signing of the pact to build the plane, and the planning had started much earlier. A strong motive linking Concorde with Suez, easily underrated, is the resentment in London and Paris of American colonialism, military and commercial. In 1956 the Sixth Fleet sailed across the Anglo-French invasion fleet as an intimidating warning, although it was actually Eisenhower's threat to bankrupt the British Treasury that ended the adventure. The last spasm of empire was over.

Since then Boeing had wrapped up the world market for jets, pioneered by the British Comet and the French Caravelle. And so, at the end of the 1950s, the French and the British decided to do something that even the Americans were wary of: to leapfrog a generation ahead, from subsonic to supersonic flight. Some of the most expert voices were skeptical. Lord Brabazon, the first man in Britain to qualify as a pilot, predicted that the Concorde's costs would be ruinous, that it would be inhumanly noisy, and that, even if it worked, all that would be achieved was that "a few businessmen might arrive two hours sooner in New York." He also pointed out, with feeling, the dismal record of the British aviation industry:

"An aircraft named after me was three years late. The engines did not arrive until three years after the project was scrapped." A prophet is not without honor . . .

At $500 million, split between the two countries, the first prediction of Concorde's costs seemed to be the price of getting Britain into the Common Market: de Gaulle, whose assent was needed, would be reassured that the British had finally turned their backs on perfidious Columbia. Even that didn't work: the British got into Europe only over the general's dead body.

The signatories of the Concorde agreement were exceptionally light-headed, even for conspirators. Costs were not discussed by the British Treasury or the French Ministry of Finance. More fatally, there was no break clause allowing either country to eject themselves in a high-speed stall. So that when Harold Wilson prepared to kill the Concorde in its tracks, he discovered that it would probably cost $500 million in the international court. By then there were all the signs of an incipient disaster: escalating costs, technical overconfidence, sloppy management. Eight years later, Roy Jenkins, Wilson's ex–aviation minister, noted ruefully, "Perhaps we should have been more stubborn even when confronted by that cliff face."

From the signing of the contract to its first flight, the Concorde ran through four governments, two Conservative and two Labour; five ministers; and, consecutively, five ministries. Its only consistency, and the reason for its resilience, lay in the management of the Custodians. Under cover of the bureaucratic mergers in Whitehall, political indetermination, and corporate voracity, the project could run fast and loose, and it did. By 1969 it had swallowed $1.8 billion; by 1972, $2.4 billion; by 1973, $2.6 billion. Parliament supinely voted the funds without being given any of the information essential for judging how it was being spent. The plane had a paralyzing power over the political will.

Certainly, technology never created a more impressive seductress. The Concorde's line is liquid and faultless to the eye, a dart to pierce the heart of sober doubt. From its needle nose to the tips of its tulip-curved wings, it seems to have consummated the aesthetics of the mind and the computer. With the nose canted down to improve the pilots' vision the Concorde has an almost anthropomorphic quality. But it has a split personality: beguiling in repose and barbaric in action. Once the four engines ignite, the earth shakes, the ears burst, the air around the plane distorts into searing bubbles of heat, and black, smearing smoke flowers into cloud and then dissipates into a cloying, sooty film. Even when it is invisible, a sliver of boiling metal at 50,000 feet, the Concorde leaves its mark on the ground in a wake of sonic boom that smashes windows and cracks walls.

The first serious rift in the display of profligate nationalism that kept the plane alive came in New York. Despite a sustained assault by French and British salesmen and politicians, Pan Am and TWA didn't buy. The salesmen were so desperate to get planes in American livery that they offered to "loan" Concordes to the airlines. That didn't work.

True Brit can turn very ugly when it is cornered. The success of Concorde demanded, it seemed, unquestioning patriotism. British air correspondents were mostly brainwashed into flag-waving support. When one of the few skeptics among them predicted cancellation of the American contractual options on Concorde, the British aerospace minister, furious with affronted patriotism, called the story "a fabrication." Within days it was confirmed. Parliament went along with the fraud. It meekly swallowed ministerial refusals to reveal what was really going on: "It would not be in the interests of the project to reveal the figures. That has been the view of every minister."

Not in *whose* interests? *The project's?*

Behind the cover-up were some strange blunders:

for example, the pilots' seats. Not, on the face of it, items of challenging technology. Originally costed at $135,000, the seats finally came out at $875,000. The Concorde crewmen will have the most pampered asses in the world.

With Pan Am and TWA out, the national-flag airlines of BOAC and Air France had to have Concorde rammed down their throats. BOAC said that operating it would bankrupt the company. It was "loaned" $324 million by the government, an offer it couldn't refuse. Even without taking that into account, the real cost of each plane delivered to BOAC and Air France, including development costs, was $533 million, a sum fit to stagger even the most hardened free spender of the military-industrial bonanza. In that way at least, the British and the French were shaping up to the Americans.

The only really tangible benefit from the Concorde was its impact on the cash flow of its two builders, the British Aircraft Corporation and Aerospatiale. That BAC made any profit at all was owing largely to the involuntary charity of the British taxpayer. BAC, as well as Concorde, was kept afloat by military contracts.

The mutability of money, notorious in all enterprises of this kind, has been greatly extended by Concorde. Just as in the cosmic measures of light-years, the familiar and mortal dimension of money cannot be translated to provide a sense of values to aerospace artifacts. The awe that strikes a man standing before an Apollo rocket is a mixture of humility and incomprehension. If told that it requires X billion dollars to encase three men in aluminum, or even half a billion dollars to provide them with as recognizable an object as a TV camera, we have to suspend all the normal faculties. This anesthetizing effect cannot be underestimated in any record like that of Concorde. Because money loses its normal dimension, the senses can be lulled so that the enormity of the experience is diminished.

Men grew old in the spell of Concorde. The chairman of BAC, Sir George Edwards, formed an early devotion to the plane that was unshakable. But in the course of ten years his face became drawn and his spirit taxed by the pressures of combating both the technical and the political problems. He didn't have much time for skeptics. At sixty-four, at the end of a distinguished career, it seemed that for him the great white bird was an albatross.

The Concorde's target date for airline service slipped back to 1976. Two years before it was due to fly its first passengers, it had cost the British taxpayers at least $1.9 billion out of a known total of $3.2 billion. Successive governments have misled Parliament on costs; each time they have had to find more money, and each time they have got it. The French have not been so reticent. On the day a British minister withheld the price being asked of airlines for the plane, it was being released to the press in Paris; on another occasion the Conservative government refused to disclose development costs, only for them to be revealed to the French Chamber of Deputies.

The French are far less furtive in their chauvinism than the British. The British felt pangs of remorse after Suez, the French merely felt betrayed by the Anglo-Saxons. In everything from atomic tests to cheese, the French national personality has hubris, however preposterous the cause. They have no need to conceal their motives, because public opinion is with them. True Brit, on the other hand, is always haunted by acts of disloyalty, always feels the skeptics snapping at its heels. The nation is not at one on its most flagrant adventures. Its rulers become mean and Draconian when responding to complaint. To complain is to be wet, to be wet is to denigrate the product, and to denigrate the product is industrial and commercial sabotage, or even treason.

The heavily censored and intermittent public reports on Concorde are peppered with weary admonitions and empty vows of reform like "revised procedures," "radical reorganization," and "investigation to remedy the defect."

One of these reports noted: "It would not be practicable or cost-effective to revise the current control system to allow monitoring of all changes." If this tone sounds familiar, it should. One of the signatures at the end of the report was that of Sir Robert Marshall, an accounting officer with a lot to account for.

The passage of Sir Robert over a decade reveals more than his own hapless destiny; it is symptomatic of the confusion and stresses in Whitehall as, one after another, the totems of Britain were put into the hands of the Custodians. Sir Robert became under-secretary at the Ministry of Aviation in 1964, just as that ministry was grappling with the appetite of Concorde. In 1966 he moved up a rung and into the Ministry of Power, where the North Sea oil contracts were administered. In 1970 he became second permanent secretary at MinTech in the last months of its life, where the Rolls-Royce story was moving toward its dénouement. MinTech was swallowed by the Department of Trade and Industry, where Sir Robert was made a Knight Commander of Britain and became, as the secretary (for industry), one of the two top civil servants—and where all the chickens were coming home to roost including the then rapacious Concorde. And in 1971 he got his KCB. (Concorde had flown through the Ministry of Aviation, the Ministry of Technology, the Ministry of Aviation Supply, the Department of Trade and Industry, and the Procurement Executive of the Ministry of Defence.) With experiences like that, Sir Robert Braithwaite Marshall needed every ounce of the faith instilled at his old public school, Sherborne, under its assertive motto: "Dieu et mon droit."

A LONG LINE OF LEMONS: ON THE ROAD WITH JOHN BULLSHIT

It was such good news that the dealers bought space in the papers to announce it: the Ford cars being sold in

Switzerland would no longer be shipped from Britain but from Germany. The models made by Ford in Britain and Cologne are outwardly identical. But they do have one hidden difference: workmanship. The British Fords left a trail of dissatisfied customers in Switzerland. The dealers' ads promised that the switch to Germany was a guarantee of "quality and impeccable finish." In the age of mass production, the human touch is still detectable.

The same thing had happened in America. The sassy Ford sports car, the Capri, is built in Britain and Germany, but the German output went to the United States because dealers complained of British workmanship. Even Henry Ford himself, launching a new Mustang model in Detroit, took time off to moan in public about sloppy work in Britain. Ford had already brusquely told Edward Heath that Britain was too risky for dependable supply. Chrysler had the same experience as Ford. It had to stop importing the small Cricket sedan from Britain because of a bad response and switched instead to Japan for its small-car imports.

Plagued though it was, British Ford is, by the standards of the country, the most skillfully managed car plant in Britain, an uncomfortable token that Detroit training was best. British Leyland, that ailing hybrid of Stokes's creation, turns out fewer than six vehicles a year per worker. Toyota turns out fifty-nine. And yet each flag-waving announcement by Stokes is greeted with the same frenzy that used to attend Nelson's victories at sea. The country *wants* to believe its own bullshit. But the British auto makers threw away the kind of chance that only comes once.

After World War II wiped out European car plants, the British had the world market at their feet. Most countries were short of dollars, and Britain's colonial network gave her access to Africa, the Middle East, and Asia as well as the noncaptive markets in Europe. By 1950 Britain exported more cars than the United States. But rather than design cars to suit foreigners, the British produced a bewildering variety of models created for the domestic snobbery of the 1930s, with fancy badges and shoddy performance. There was little after-sales backup. Instead of winning markets, these lemons poisoned the well.

By 1956 Germany was able to overtake Britain as the top car exporter, virtually on the reputation of the Beetle alone. Between 1964 and 1970 British auto exports slumped from 21.7 percent of the world market to 13.4 percent. The Japanese followed the Germans in wiping up the world business and then joined them in cleaning up in the British home market, where both are now strongly established.

Nearly a third of the cars now sold in Britain are foreign-made. A half of the industry is American-owned. Becoming desperate under this pressure, Lord Stokes called for restrictions on imports, but it was too late. One of Stokes's own spokesmen had said "safety is bad box office," acknowledging that the cars they shipped to the United States had to be heavily modified to meet the far more stringent safety and emission standards. The British market was more tolerant.

British exports now depend largely on either luxury or sports cars. Neither is an idea created for foreign markets. Both happen to be British specialties filling gaps left by conventional mass production. And both depend more and more on mystique rather than a sense of value for money. The anxiety to own a piece of mobile True Brit is very forgiving. Take, for example, that different breed of cat, the Jaguar.

The Jaguar has always been as much a cult as a car. It has the aura of the thoroughbred. But there are really two Jaguars, the one in the mind, with an assist from the adman, and the one in the garage. In America the Jaguar is sold as a specialized "road car," a tonic for the uncertain libido. Besides its sexual equipment, the Jaguar is also regarded as a piece of hand-crafted machinery.

In truth, the Jaguar is a brilliantly designed car made in an aging and overstrained plant. Both before and after it passed into the ragbag of British Leyland, the company has been so undercapitalized that it could never meet demand. This pressure to turn out more cars in spite of the plant has dimmed the passions of many a buck as, en route to some idyllic assignation, an expensive noise erupts from somewhere in the works.

In Britain, Jaguar's image has moved away from the passion wagon to satisfying the more bourgeois urges of the business executive who wants the comforts of a sedan with a tinge of the sports car, rather like a wistfully flickering memory of pleasures past and fruits long since picked. The XJ12 sedan caught this demand so perfectly that the company's previous underestimates of demand seem in comparison to be minor. The plant could crank out only 120 XJ 12s a week (when it was not strike-bound), creating such a scarcity value that a black market developed. A secondhand XJ12 sold for $13,125—$3,800 over the British list price. Many British customers thought the car was *underpriced*—in other words, not exclusive enough. Jaguar exploited this snobbery in an ad: "We're doing all we can to stop the car falling into the wrong hands, so that people like you can enjoy the ecstasy without the agony of waiting too long or paying more than you should." The waiting list ran anything up to two years, a long while for those sublimated satyrs who make the Jaguar such a hot property.

BUY ME, I'M THE REAL TRUE BRIT

Lured into humiliation by the Impossible Dream, and leaving a trail of lemons on the roads of the world, True Brit is left in the marketplace secure only with a sentimental kind of appeal distilled—if that is not too much of a pun—in the world of the whiskey ads. Whiskey is so near to being a God-given essence (try Japanese whiskey and see how divine that is) that it would take real genius to louse it up. But the glass of whiskey has been parlayed by the ad agency photographers into something that wraps up a way of life—drink the stuff and you turn into True Brit. . . .

The man is probably in his country tweeds. He has a way of leaning on the palings of the horse farm so that the creases all fall right. He'll be wearing his flat tweed cap; the important thing about the cap is the way his hair falls out from under. Generations of barbering have gone into the cut of that hair. A True Briton has always worn his hair just a little bit long at the back. They cut it like that at Eton, although the True Briton probably never went to Eton. There used to be something slightly, well— slightly *faggy* about that hair, flopping over the collar at the back. But not anymore.

In his selling mode, the True Briton has companions, three of them. A horse, a dog, and a woman, in that order. The horse is a thoroughbred, probably stud. The woman has also been carefully bred, just like the horse, to be dumb but elegant. She has one of those long white necks, one string of pearls. One for class, two for flash, three for bad taste. Only women in the royal family who don't know any better wear three strings of pearls. She also wears sensible shoes. Sensible shoes are more than shoes, they are a state of mind. The impress of *control*. Sensible shoes know how far to go, and they will never go further. At least, not in a whiskey ad.

The dog is probably an Irish setter. Dogs and horses are two of the things the Irish do well. The True Briton is very careful about the Irish: he won't touch their whiskey and he'll seldom touch their women. But the dogs and the horses—they can be made to behave.

In this role the True Briton is truly himself. He is

not overreaching, he is not out of character, he can handle it. Whether it's whiskey, pottery, fake antiques, men's clothes, sensible shoes, sporting guns—all the accouterments of his decadent tastes—then you can trust him. He knows those games, they are a part of his breeding, the stamp of his class. But if he appears as the new *Wunderkind* of technology, keep your distance. He's not himself.

11. CULTURAL DEFOLIATION

"You Can All Kiss Good-bye to a New Piccadilly Circus"

Even the most casual visitor to London cannot help but notice that Piccadilly Circus is a semiderelict slum. Superficially it seems a victim of the same kind of blight that has struck Times Square. Tacky porno shops, skin movies, pinball arcades, and toxic hamburger joints are all around it. In the center, once supposed to be the center both of the empire and of the world, the island bearing Eros has been chopped away for the convenience of traffic. Behind neon facades the buildings are flaking and unkempt. But what seems to be the attrition of urban nihilism is not. Piccadilly Circus is a pawn in an elaborate game plan that has made a few men rich and at the same time has eaten away the historic roots of London more insidiously than any cancer.

London is not the only capital to fall victim to the rapacity of the property speculator. But the difference between London and most other victims is that, each time a building is demolished, an irreplaceable piece of history is likely to go with it. Not only is London extremely vulnerable to this kind of cultural defoliation, but it is also the home and training ground of a band of men who have set out to raze other cities across the world. One of Britain's successful exports is a highly sophisticated technique for turning destruction into gold.

London lacks the martial perspectives of Paris, the baroque chaos of Rome. It's an unplanned city, assembled piecemeal with history piled like silt along its streets. Invading Roman armies chose its site in A.D. 43. By the year 190 the Romans had built a walled city on the north bank of the Thames, and those walls still define what is now the City of London, temple of Mammon, and, ironically, the engine of the old London's destruction. Modern London still follows the street plan of Stuart London. Until this century that plan determined the city's perspectives and scale; the texture of London was all of a piece. Without the imposition of a grand design, it was coherent. In a thousand years a city rich in character had been built.

After Hitler's demolition work, the first wave of postwar reconstruction, from the late forties to the mid-fifties, exposed the bankruptcy of modern British architecture. The crime was aesthetic, not venal. The second wave, from the late fifties to the mid-sixties, was different. The demand was for offices, and it transformed cubic blocks of air space into fortunes for developers, who were allowed to bulldoze away priceless historic buildings. But there was a third assault, and this marked a new kind of manipulation that did for property development what asset-stripping did simultaneously to industry. It transformed nominal values into astronomical ones. This game was devised and executed by a relatively small number of people.

There are three steps in it. The first is to identify the most valuable sites and then acquire them with such stealth that the people selling the separate parts are kept ignorant of their real value. The second is to negotiate with planning authorities a scheme to maximize the rentable space. Having thus assembled not just a building but a machine capable virtually of printing money, the final step is what might be called Chinese bookkeeping: borrowing the finance for construction with the planning permission as sufficient collateral, then capitalizing the scheme on its realizable income. It is an ingenious technique involving a marginal outlay, no risk, and stupendous profits. There were peculiar reasons why it worked in London better than anyplace else.

Office space was already at a premium in the early sixties, but the Labour government, in one of its most counterproductive strokes, turned a good thing into a bonanza. They slapped a limit on office developments, which, after a deadline, depended on getting tightly controlled permits. With the supply curtailed, the rent per square foot in central London went from $6.80 in 1964 to $16.00 in 1970. Although the restraints were then modified, the escalation continued. By 1973 prime space in the City of London was nearly $50 a square foot—five times the current price in Manhattan. The capital value of an office block is put at twenty times the annual rent it produces. For one London scheme alone, this meant a capital value of at least $500 million on construction costs of $112 million.

With pickings of this size, a juggernaut was let loose. Property development in central London bore no relation to social need and no mercy for the city's vulnerable historical fabric. The city's legislators and administrators, the only people with the power to contain and control redevelopment, were babes in arms when confronted by the guile and blandishments of the speculators. Planning officers were conned into surrendering key sites in return for peanuts—tower blocks seemed to do something for their ego. The city was being robbed, by consent.

The memorial to this philosophy and age is a thirty-four-story office tower called Centre Point, which dominates the skyline of London's West End. It was built in 1964 but stayed empty for ten years. Not because it was a lemon, but because it was worth more empty than full. The man who built it, a bearded autocrat called Harry Hyams, was simply waiting for the market to meet his price—$2.5 million a year. Until it did, with 202,000 square feet of space appreciating year by year, Hyams could afford to wait. The London boom had made him a personal fortune of $750 million. Centre Point itself, built for $10 million, had in a decade become worth $100 million. This asset value was the seed corn of all Hyams's other speculations.

Stung by Hyams's colossal nerve, Peter Walker saw Centre Point as a blemish on his new capitalism. He told Parliament, "The time has come to bring an end to this highly undesirable practice." Hyams's response was to advertise the building in European newspapers as "the best-known office building in the world." But notoriety was not enough. There were still no takers. And Peter Walker could huff and puff but he couldn't blow Centre Point down, or do anything about Hyams's arrogant stratagem.

The struggle between property speculators and city legislators is an unequal one. In other countries the conjunction of such an opportunity for vast personal gain and the relatively modest means of the men dispensing the license to make that gain would create the perfect conditions for graft. It can, as we shall see, also work out that way in Britain. But naïveté is in some ways more of a vice than corruption. The smart property speculator in

London can say with some truth, "When things go so well without corruption, why introduce it?"

Property speculation in London brings into play, on the one side, planning officers (many not even trained planners) earning about $7,500 a year and, on the other side, a number of men wearing camel's-hair coats who run Rolls-Royces with TV for the rear seats and who can pick up a clear $1 million or more a year. The planning officer has little commercial sophistication. He is probably highly scrupulous, a pedant about zoning laws, and socially very impressionable. It is not corruption. It is the intercourse, familiar in Britain, of the amateur and the professional.

It is Piccadilly Circus, the hub of the universe, that shows what happens when the jackals group in the undergrowth around a promising carcass. From 1959 the Circus was a battleground for the competing fashions of urban planning and architecture. The first developer to see its potential for self-enrichment was Jack Cotton, the man who dropped the Pan Am building across Park Avenue to block out the sky. Cotton's plans were undermined by a counterattack by aesthetes. No deep popular sentiment was aroused. A succession of alternatives, each reflecting the fads of their time, were proposed for the Circus: bigger roads; "piazzas"; overhead pedestrian "walkways"; neon-girdled "entertainment complexes."

By 1965 speculators had quietly prospected and bought up the three major blocks available for redevelopment on the fringe of the Circus. The fancier ideas had given way to hard commercial logic. One plan included 544,000 square feet of office space calculated to make a profit of $69 million. This was the brainchild of Joe Levy, one of the founding fathers of the London boom. Levy's plan was so flagrant that the legislators acceded to public uproar and promised, at least, to limit the height of the new buildings to that of the old. But people like Levy and Hyams don't take kindly to having their wings clipped. If the legislators didn't go along with him, Levy warned, "you can all kiss good-bye to a new Piccadilly Circus."

Although the name of the game was exposed in Piccadilly, its ultimate scope was understood by very few Londoners. Demolition and redevelopment are dispersed and involve a time lapse. The dimensions of the London defoliation are staggering both in what has already been done and in what will be done. In the City of London alone, where the layers of history are at their deepest, 130 major sites went ahead simultaneously. More than a quarter of the City's archaeological deposits have been destroyed by the digging of deep basements. There is no legal requirement to consider archaeological value before development. The work of centuries in which buildings were shaped to the needs of people is being interred by the needs of the fast buck. Less than a fifth of the material evidence for Roman, Saxon, and medieval London survives; in twenty years it will have gone.

In the London that in little more than a decade created a new crop of multimillionaires, a quarter of the housing stock is structurally condemned. In the inner belt two-thirds of the homes were built before the end of World War I, most of them between 1875 and 1919. These are not buildings that merit preservation other than as examples of the squalor that was socially acceptable to the Victorians and Edwardians. There are 250,000 houses lacking basic facilities like indoor sanitation. Legislators bemused by the "prestige" of office blocks and hungry for the taxes they generate have been cynically tardy in sweeping away these slums.

The ten largest property companies in Britain control assets of about $7.5 billion—more than the entire gold and dollar reserves of the country. Joe Levy, like Harry Hyams, had stacked up profits of over $100 million by 1972 and was not acting like a satisfied man. Hyams's architect, a fiddle-playing former army officer called Colonel Richard Seifert, has had more influence on the London skyline than Wren, but with rather less distinction. Still, he can laugh all the way to the bank. His company has a turnover of more than $125 million a year.

But London will not be the sole beneficiary of British developers and speculators. By 1973 British firms had $1.5 billion of office blocks under way in Europe. In Brussels alone there were thirty-five towers to commemorate British enterprise. In Paris a British developer, having made a killing among the innocent there by using the London Method, predicted that they would have to ease up. The natives were rising. Even in New York, following the early precedent of the Pan Am building, British developers sniffed opportunity. The old country still had one or two kinds of colonialism left to play.

Six hundred and fifty miles north of London you come to the end of the British Isles, at the island of Unst. This is one of the Shetland Islands, with a hundred miles of sea between them and the northern tip of Scotland. Around the serrated shoreline of Unst the Atlantic meets the North Sea. It is farther north than Leningrad, and on the same latitude as Anchorage, Alaska. But thanks to the Gulf Stream, Unst is frost-free in the winter. (Without the Gulf Stream, Britain's climate would equal Labrador's.) Despite this, no trees grow on Unst and the winds cut through anything but stone. The place names are a blend of Celtic and Nordic: Uyeasound, Mu Ness, Muckle Flugga, and Baltasound.

This is the land of the Norsemen. A Scandinavian king traded the Shetlands to Scotland in 1471, and by the devolutions of warfare the Shetlanders ended up being called British. But nothing farther from the urban refinements of London is imaginable. Until the 1970s the eight hundred inhabitants of Unst were self-sustaining and independent; there was no unemployment, and the only problem was a trickling wastage of the younger people toward the city lights a few hundred miles and a world away to the south. Twentieth-century blights passed Unst by. The only callers were mainly fishermen: Norwegians, Danes, Faroese, and Icelanders running for shelter from storms into Unst's tiny harbor of Norwick. The island's one bar was apt to see its whiskey reserves vanish overnight.

For people at peace with the world and needing none of its more contrived pleasures, Unst was as near Utopian as the spirit could crave. Then came the oilmen. The two basins running to the east and west of the Shetlands are probably the richest oil deposits of the new bonanza. The cloud over the composure of the Shetlands is affluence. An early estimate of what the oil business could be worth to the Shetlands was $25 million a year. From a condition of thrifty contentment, the seventeen thousand Shetlanders have the prospect of becoming one of Britain's richest communities. But there is a price to be paid.

Of the three main Shetland Islands, Unst is the least impressed by the prospects of a fortune from oil. Its traditional sources of income, fishing and crofting, are tough but automatically self-selecting. Nobody works like that unless they enjoy it. Fish-processing is the Shetlands' main industry, but on Unst this smacks too much of organized activity. Fishing, crofting, and breeding Shetland ponies are closer to God. Supporting the needs of oil companies is something else. But elsewhere in the Shetlands people are less immune to temptation. Even the smallest bureaucracy becomes devious when financial gain is put into jeopardy by the normal democratic processes.

Four oil companies, Shell, Exxon, British Petroleum, and Conoco coveted the Shetlands as the nearest landfall to their new wells. They wanted new harbors, storage tanks, and a refinery. The refinery would be one of the biggest in Europe: 650 acres. It would be run with a staff of six hundred and would need five thousand imported workmen to build it. The total Shetlands labor force is only three thousand.

A thirty-three-strong county council governs the Shetlands. Within the council a committee in control of planning swiftly became a pro-oil lobby. In six months the price of land around the Shetland capital of Lerwick rose from $2,500 an acre to $10,000 an acre and kept rising. There was only one problem in the path of this boom: people. In places like Baltasound on Unst, selected as a site for a harbor and storage depot, those living the simple life of honest labor were in the way. In one croft, for example, a young widow scratched out a meager living with poultry and vegetables, but still felt uninclined to move aside for the bulldozer. Others also resisted, aware of the "modifications" of the landscape proposed to accommodate the oil industry. The reluctant widow and her allies were regarded by the council oil caucus as shortsighted and obstructionist, the kind of epithets used by zealous administrators the world over. Bureaucrats impeded in this way turn their mind to law, and if the law is uncooperative they turn their mind to making new law.

The sixteen Shetlanders inside the oil caucus decided to set up a Port and Harbor Authority. It would be empowered by law to remove people in the path of progress. It would be able to purchase compulsorily the holdings of stubborn widows, giving only twenty-eight days' notice before the bulldozers moved in. The price paid would be at the authority's discretion. The "master plan" for the authority was drawn up by consulting engineers in London at a cost of $175,000. Nobody on the Shetland Islands but the oil lobby saw these plans, although the oil companies were consulted. The politics of the Shetlands, until then placidly parochial, began to show all the signs of cosmopolitan intrigue. They attracted the energies of oilmen, consulting engineers, developers, and numerous parasites who, at the first whiff of oil in the nostrils, flock to the scene. Men measured the price of other men.

Once every two weeks the bank arrives on Unst, weather permitting. The bank is a man with a suitcase full of bills from the five Scottish banks. Money has so far played a modest part in that spartan life. But the oil is coming.

Environmentalism, that slovenly word, is a fashion. The barbarism it faces is a tradition. Beautiful buildings have been thoughtlessly destroyed by each generation's needs and sense of its own superiority. The British invented the Industrial Revolution, and they have been as mindless as anyone of its by-products. Industrial pollution began in the Elysian dales of Derbyshire. The heart of England was clawed out to feed the furnace of Mammon. As the innovator, Britain now has the world's worst legacy of industrial wreckage: deposits of burned-out industries, ravaged land, and exhausted people.

You can measure this by the eye, but scarcely in the mind. More than a quarter of a million acres of land in England and Wales, where land is precious, is classified as "derelict." This is really dead land, consumed and discarded. It can offer life to nothing else. It is barren and toxic. These vast wastes do not include the industrial slums: in 1973 there were still two and a half million people in England and Wales living in houses classified by the euphemism of "unfit," lacking one or all of the basic amenities of hot water, bathtub, or indoor toilet. In many cities the conditions are getting worse, not better.

The most neglected areas are the seedbeds of industrialism. In the north of England 16 percent of the homes have outside toilets, compared to 7 percent in the southeast. The worst conditions are in Scotland, where things have been so bad for so long that the population is draining south. In Glasgow, a city without a center or a soul, the population has shrunk from 1.2 million in 1945 to 900,000 in 1972 and is still falling, at the rate of 25,000 a year.

The worst pollution and the worst housing coincide, afflicting the most defenseless and the poorest people: the working class marooned in the discarded debris of the nineteenth-century industrial baronies. New "clean" industries and their white-collar workers are outside the dying cities. The two unhealthiest regions, measured by the incidence of deaths from lung cancer, heart disease, and bronchitis are northwest England and Scotland—the places containing the most abject slums. The highest levels of lead contamination in the blood of children are in the urban working-class neighborhoods.

This human and physical degradation ought to be the most sobering restraint on flights of megatheres like Concorde and the pouring of public funds into new airports and the Channel Tunnel. But when social remedy and commercial interests compete in Britain, the real priorities become clear. Official "policy" reveals the dichotomy. The Department of the Environment is little better than a cynical exercise in tokenism. The Department of Trade and Industry, with totally opposing interests and values, has the clout. The conflict was exquisitely embodied in one man: Peter Walker.

Walker was the first environment minister—the first in the world, as he pointed out to an international conference of conservationists. The ministry is, in truth, a sham piece of window dressing covering the convenience of a bureaucratic merger of transport, planning, and local-government administration. Walker found no conflict in moving across to head the DTI; one day the gamekeeper, the next the poacher. He showed the same agility in business. While the Environment Ministry neglects the slums, the DTI sponsors a new phase of industrial rape. It is funding with $125 million the commercial exploration of British mineral deposits.

This is not just a generous subsidy to already rich companies (Rio Tinto Zinc, an immediate beneficiary, made profits of $297 million in 1973) in the form of a 35 percent chunk of exploration costs. It is a frontal assault on a treasured national asset. The remaining minerals of any worth are mostly in the national parks. Less than $2.5 million a year is spent on maintaining the parks; with the government subsidy, about $250 million is being spent on mineral exploration.

By the 1980s it is estimated $250 million worth of nonferrous metal can be mined in Britain, a sixth of the country's imports. But the bulk of this would have to come from the national parks. An open-cast mine for nonferrous metals covers 1,500 acres and needs 3,000 more acres for surrounding activity. The metals are some of the most poisonous to man, animals, and plants.

Peter Walker talked of "a new age of elegance for the mass of the people," about as meaningful as his "new capitalism" was for the people. As a policing agent, the Environment Ministry is a fraud; the housing department was caught trying to cover its bad record by "fixing" parliamentary questions in its favor; the transport department has a reputation for excessive secrecy and for ruthlessly overriding environmental objections to road plans. One of Walker's first acts was to announce one thousand miles of new expressways.

Industrial pollution is policed by a body with the archaic title of the Alkali Inspectorate. To cover the whole country there are thirty inspectors. In half a century the inspectorate brought three prosecutions. The inspectors don't like to be thought of as policemen but as educators. They are True Believers in the British Way. Their chief boasted, "The Americans take a big stick and threaten. . . . We say to industry, 'Look, lads, *we've* got a problem.'" Since 1967 the prosecutions have speeded up. To two a year. The fines are $250 a time.

The sceptered isle, set in a silver sea, is being systematically poisoned. Like the air and the land, the sea and the rivers are employed as the rectum of industry. In one summer 100,000 seabirds, mostly guillemots, were killed by dumped chemicals in the waters off western Britain. A survey of thirty-two British coastal resorts shows that thirty-one of them discharge their sewage into the sea. In rivers, 60 percent of the sewage and 50 percent of the effluents are discharged illegally. In 1971 the average fine for oil spillage from tankers was $500. In spite of tougher legislation, ninety convictions in one year totaled only $55,000 in fines.

12. FIDDLERS FIND THEIR FEET

Building Brasilia in the Frozen North

Two things, above all others, are distributed unequally in Britain: wealth, and the weather. Nearly a third of the British live where both are found at their most generous, in London and the southeast. This area is called the Golden Triangle.

Three hundred miles to the northeast lie Yorkshire, Durham, and Northumberland. For a good part of the year these counties are regarded by Londoners as the frozen north. In this exposed and flinty land some of the worst Victorian industrial slums survive, around the shipyards of the Tyne and Tees, the fishing ports of the Humber, the woollen and steel mills of Yorkshire, and the coal mines of Durham. In the 1960s the northeast still had the worst housing in England; industrial pollution was twice as bad as London's; unemployment was high. And yet the people hung on, the population stayed steady.

In spite of being crowded on a small island, the British are not a homogeneous people. Regions are like separate races. The hardy northeasterners, layered by dialects and allegiances, are as different from Londoners as are Danes from Parisians, and they have their own culture. In Yorkshire, it's rugby football, cricket, and the earthy, hard-boozing circuit of the workingmen's clubs; well-heeled middle-class merchants declining flash in favor of the freemasonry of Conservative Clubs and comforts hidden behind stone walls; a parchment-skinned gentry in the expansive Brontë country; landed aristos ranging the grouse moors.

In Newcastle, something else: the "Geordies," soccer-crazy and randy, with some of the hardest criminals and gamiest clubs outside Soho. If there is any common denominator of character in this varied territory, it is clannishness—classes sealed in their own orbits, self-sustaining and self-protective through discreet chains of personal contact. Though the middle class and the aristos hold their ground, literally, one party dominates this region's politics to the point where it is almost a substate of the nation: Labour. Most of the town, city, and county legislatures are run by the Labour party. Most parliamentary constituencies return massive Labour majorities.

The first people to make an administrative entity of northeast England were the Romans, but only after a lot of trouble. Its importance as a province of Roman Britain lay in the need to establish and defend the border with Scotland, where the stubborn Caledonians met Roman culture with barbarism. It took the Romans a century and a half to secure and establish the province under the name of Northumbria. The Roman difficulties were not caused primarily by the Caledonians, though they were bad enough, but by a savage local tribe called the Brigantes. Civilizing this wild bunch turned out to be one of the most tiring tests of the Latin conquerors. The Brigantes viewed the ways of Rome with much the same contempt as their twentieth-century descendants view London. Though finally subdued, their name lives on in the word *brigand* (derived from the same root), tribute to their freebooting and marauding style.

In 1964 the old province of Northumbria was high in the priorities of Harold Wilson's first Labour administration. In a marginal election result the region's loyal party battalions came out in force, and due reward had to be paid. Ailing industries like shipbuilding had somehow to be revived; new industry, which preferred the Golden Triangle, had to be "redirected" north; the great blots of urban squalor had to be replaced by whole new towns. Northumbria was set for a boom.

At Wilson's elbow was a man with a vision. T. Dan Smith was one of the election tacticians. He wanted a role in the Northumbrian revival. He was ideal material. Smith was the son of a Durham miner and had risen rapidly in the northeastern Labour party. Like Richard Daley's Chicago Democratic organization, the network of Northumbrian Labour party councils operates with the clout of a traditional and unshakable captive vote. Party caucuses are oligarchic, the fief of commited men. To anybody without a political bent, without a taste for local power, it seems prosaic and thankless work. Many of the politicians are manual workers, as close to the soul of the Labour movement as you can get, and a good deal closer than many of the Labour M.P.'s at Westminster.

It is almost another party, this tightly knit and essentially federalized system, and nowhere is it more in control than the northeast. This is the Labour party that T. Dan Smith knew by every vein, through which he had matured into the first British politician to be compared with an American big-city boss. It was a comparison that Smith encouraged. The American use of bigness was something that he approved of and actively emulated. Dreaming on the big scale, planning with a greater sweep than the parochial obsessions normal in British local politics, seeing power as cumulative and socially decisive—this was the vision of T. Dan Smith.

In 1960 Smith became the Labour leader of Newcastle upon Tyne and was dubbed "Mr. Newcastle." It was the kind of power base he needed and knew how to use. It gave him national visibility, and it gave him influence with and access to the top reaches of the party. He talked of building a Brasilia in the north, of importing the architecture of Corbusier and Arne Jacobsen. Picking up another American technique, Smith used public relations as an implement of political persuasion. Influence-peddling and power brokerage could, Smith saw, be updated and refined under the euphemism of public relations. Soon he was running five PR companies.

In Westminster Smith was regarded as a phenomenon, a man of altogether higher caliber than the normal run of city factotums. He was careful not to be influenced by the middle-class airs of London socialism. He wore ill-fitting and unfashionable double-breasted suits, and his hair was not so much barbered as chopped in the crude provincial style. His one concession to trend was to wear the same brand of raincoat as Harold Wilson, a Gannex with tartan lapels.

Pontefract is a small Yorkshire town on the southern fringe of Northumbria. Nothing very much distinguishes it. Richard II died in its Norman castle; it has a good racetrack; it is known for an evil medallion-shaped liquorice candy called Pontefract Cake. One guidebook, hard-pressed to flatter the place, lists an "impressive power station." Among the thirty thousand citizens of Pontefract there are no famous favorite sons. But for a decade or so the town will enjoy a marginal celebrity as the home of an architect called John Poulson. Fiddling came of age in Pontefract, and Poulson was its Leonardo.

At the age of twenty the precocious Poulson, without any formal training, set up shop as an architect in Pontefract. By 1960, at the age of fifty, he was a model citizen of his community. His business thrived, he was a nabob of the local Methodist church, a worshipful master of two local Freemasonry lodges and provincial grand deacon of the Freemasons' regional branch, and chairman of the National Liberal wing of the local Conservative party. He was even a lay commissioner of the Internal Revenue Department. Not only were these impressive credentials—they showed that Poulson knew astutely how the local system worked.

His Freemasonry was especially significant. This is a quasi-secret society, absurdly ritualistic, but very effective as a covert way of doing business. Plugged into that network, nominally apolitical, and able at the same time to deal among the Tory hierarchy, Poulson had good reason to feel a securely self-made man. Soon after Edward Heath became leader of the Tories, Poulson appeared at his side at a local meeting and told him, "Our respect for you is our recognition of your personal integrity, a quality sadly lacking in many who are engaged in public life today."

By that time the Labour government was pumping millions of pounds of aid into the northeast, and the money materialized mostly in the form of new building. As well as public housing, the local councils wanted new schools, hospitals, swimming pools, and office blocks for their burgeoning bureaucracies. It was a building spree, and John Poulson was well placed to get a big piece of the action.

T. Dan Smith became chairman of the Northern Economic Planning Council in 1965, the primary instrument of Wilson's redevelopment program. "Mr. Newcastle" was now "Mr. Northumbria." Poulson had had an office in Newcastle since 1962; his own empire had extended to national and international projects. Poulson was in no doubt about who was the man to see in Newcastle. He hired the Smith PR network to promote his work to local councils. Two of the prohibitions enforced by the Royal Institute of British Architects are touting or soliciting for business and involvement in building companies.

If the first rule were literally enforced, any architect without previous work to his credit would find it virtually impossible to break into the business. In practice, few architects are as self-denying as this. But what Poulson did went a good deal further than making casual business contacts. Smith knew how local government worked, he knew that municipal building programs were awash with funds, and he could give Poulson leverage in towns and cities where he was still unknown. Smith *was* leverage. And he was ready to help Poulson, at a price.

With Smith's assistance, Poulson built up a biographical index on local legislators. The two men also joined together in a company aimed at introducing to Britain a Scandinavian concept for prefabricated housing, which, along with Utopian architecture, was an enthusiasm of Smith's. This company was called Open System Building, and it was destined to reach into the British political stratosphere.

In the early 1960s Reginald Maudling was among the few likely candidates to succeed to the leadership of the Conservative party. The major mark against him was an indelible impression of lethargy: he is a great rambling, untidy hulk of a man with epicurean girth, a ready grin, and sardonic humor. What was missing was the cold and hungry eye of Edward Heath and the Hustlers, the sign of the non-wet. Reggie Maudling doesn't hustle, he shambles like an overweight prizefighter who would rather sink back into the corner and take the bell. Maudling lost out to Heath for the leadership. But when John Poulson recruited him he was still high in the party councils and a very substantial catch.

With Maudling's international reputation as the draw, Poulson appointed him chairman of two of his companies. Later he made him a director of Open System Building and paid $20,000 a year into a favorite charity of Mrs. Maudling's. Two of Maudling's small sons were shareholders in a Poulson company, and their elder brother was a director. Maudling was extraordinarily unwary of his patron. He didn't even realize that professional ethics were being flouted by an architect running a firm like Open System Building. And he was painstakingly obliging in small things, like helping to book a $450 winter cruise for a senior civil servant and his wife, a gift from Poulson.

By this time Poulson had the biggest architectural practice in Europe, with 750 employees and offices in major British cities and in Beirut and Lagos. But there was something peculiar about the accounts. In 1967 Poulson's fees were $2.9 million, but he recorded a profit of only $225,725. Since Poulson was paying himself at the rate of about $250,000 a year, the business was not as sound as it seemed. On the surface Poulson exuded the kind of confident success rare in the experience of Pontefract: a Rolls-Royce, expensive suits, silk ties, and an expansive manner. He had a reputation for being generous. But although he gave no sign of knowing it, Poulson's empire had overreached itself and was on the rocks.

Smith, meantime, went from strength to strength. He was appointed to a royal commission to plan the reorganization of the whole of British local government. He was also the chairman of two development corporations assigned to build entire new cities in the northeast. Smith had no inkling that his client and business partner was in financial straits, though he had ample reason to know of Poulson's openhandedness. Apart from more formal contracts between them, Poulson paid for Smith and his family to take vacations in Italy, Majorca, and Greece; one cost at least $1,000.

But Smith was not alone in getting gifts and favors from Poulson. All over Northumbria, legislators, civil servants, and executives in state utilities were wined and dined by the architect. Many also got donations in cash. Poulson's foundering business owed its emergence from obscurity to international prominence very largely to one discovery: the latent venality of British local government. More than anyone could have imagined possible, Poulson dropped small measures of temptation into the system and watched them grow into a pervasive rot.

From about 1960, when Poulson began hiring politicians and civil servants as "consultants," the greased palm was the key to his success. Most of his soft touches were low-salaried men; one or two were struggling to find any work at all. Their use lay in their unpaid political posts. Others were classic cases of galloping corruption, men of adequate means who just wanted to live more lavishly, like a senior Scottish civil servant who built a $50,000 house with Poulson's help, and had a $5,000 sedan from him. Most of the graft, though, was petty, and some of it was pathetic.

Vacations in the sun were a seductive charity to sick men at the end of obscure careers who wanted to escape with their wives from the rheumatic inhospitality of Northumbria and lacked any means of doing so. One slip of this kind was enough to tarnish a life of previously unblemished public service. It was a temptation that Poulson knew how to use. But when somebody failed to come through, he was rapidly discarded. A letter from Poulson to Smith wrote off one legislator as "the strong man for years who is losing his grip"; another was called "a broken reed." By Poulson's lights the useful were to be used and the weak quickly dropped.

The agent of the downfall of John Poulson was not any of the law-enforcement agencies. They had not caught so much as a sniff of his odor. It was the jackals of the Internal Revenue who got on his tail. In 1968 they claimed over $400,000 from him in unpaid taxes. Even this process took nearly four years to flush out the true character of Poulson's business. When it did, fiddling became an established fact, and a seismic shock ran through British politics and local government.

The scandal burned with a slow fuse. The tax claim precipitated a declaration of bankruptcy. This meant a public "examination in bankruptcy" to locate the cause of insolvency, fix the liabilities of the debtor, and seek to recover what was owing to creditors. It was a job for a patient army of investigators. In Poulson's Pontefract offices alone there were six tons of files.

Poulson admitted liabilities of $617,000. Hearings for bankruptcy are normally as enthralling as a public reading of a mortgage agreement or a telephone directory. Newspapers tend to ignore them. This was the case when the Poulson hearings opened. Reporters had to be prodded by a more vigilant arm of the press.

Maudling was the most prominent casualty of the Poulson affair. But his connection with Poulson was exposed first in the London satirical magazine *Private Eye*. Maudling was deputy prime minister and home secretary in the Heath government, responsible, among other things, for the police. As long as the liability of having worked for Poulson seemed only to have been an association with incompetence, Maudling did not see any reason to be compromised by it—nor did his colleagues in the cabinet. None of them liked *Private Eye,* since no politician esteems a muckraker. Maudling's sin seemed his gullibility in joining the Poulson empire in the first place. But Reggie the Unwary was trapped. When it became clear that strange things were visible under a stone only partially prised up, Scotland Yard's Fraud Squad took an interest. With the police involved, Maudling had to resign. Like others, some still under cover, Maudling saw his career punctured by the ingratiating John Poulson.

The counsel for the creditors, Mr. Muir Hunter,

Q.C., circled Poulson as a great predatory bird might
slowly tease a rabbit before disemboweling it. His accent
was in the best public-school manner, tinged with simu-
lated incredulity:

> So you and Mr. Maudling, both persons afflicted by the
> cares of state and business, were occupying yourselves with
> booking, a year in advance, a cruise for an elderly civil ser-
> vant. Is that what you have spent most of your time on,
> you and Mr. Maudling?

Poulson was dressed for the hearings like a man
whose wife had given him the last flick with the clothes
brush, straightened his tie, viewed the fall of his cuffs,
checked his grooming, and pronounced him fit for public
inspection. There was not a fleck of dust on him. His pate
was bald and as polished as the rest of him. His dark eyes
were steady, his bearing that of a man who is hearing for
the very first time that he has been systematically milked.
When Muir Hunter revealed that between 1962 and 1970
Poulson had paid out $387,000 to T. Dan Smith, Poul-
son's response was: "Phew!"

As a good Freemason, Poulson was not prepared to
delve into the purpose of public relations as practiced by
T. Dan Smith. He had been careless, muddled, and, of
course, magnanimous. During eight years he had dis-
bursed $819,822 for various services rendered, including
the money paid to Smith. As Muir Hunter commented:
"Now it is plain, is it not, Mr. Poulson, that you are a man
with an immensely generous heart: is that not right?"

"I used to think so. I think now, when I see these figures, stupid would describe it."

Poulson presented himself as the victim.

But others began to squirm. One minister had already fallen, other M.P.'s had been named. For once it
was no use the Labour party taking its normal sanctimo-
nious line about the endemic graft of capitalism: their
own rebuilding program had generated gravy, and most

of the cormorants attracted to it were minor Labour officials. Even an innocent and trivial gift from Poulson, like a coffeepot given to a Labour minister when he officially opened a Poulson-designed school, got headline attention. "All I want is to get rid of the bloody thing," said the pursued minister. Reginald Maudling, after Muir Hunter delved into his correspondence with Poulson, complained, "They can say what they bloody well like about me, and I don't get a chance to reply."

Maudling's discomfort reflected sensitive nerves in high places. The unorthodox method of disclosure, where there were no criminal charges and yet where shit hit the fan every day, was regarded as a lapse in the standards of the club—not by Poulson, *but by Muir Hunter*. According to this view, reputations of public men were being traduced. Scant regard would be paid to such feelings had the "reputations" been those of the Northumbrian small fry, but bigger fish were involved.

The bankruptcy laws had last been overhauled in 1914, which by British standards makes them newly minted. But nothing makes law obsolete as fast as an endangered elite. Suddenly the Heath government decided that the rules governing bankruptcy hearings needed review. The chief law officer, the lord chancellor, was, he told the House of Lords, "considering amending the rules so as to underline the court's powers to exclude *irrelevant or scandalous matter* and to order that such matter be excluded from the record."

This uncharacteristic celerity in dealing with legal reform was revealed a day before the failure of an attempt to get Muir Hunter to adopt a more respectful style of interrogation in the bankruptcy court. After complaints in Parliament about the handling of Poulson, the Professional Conduct Committee of the Bar Council (the self-policing mechanism of the lawyers) announced an inquiry into Muir Hunter's "conduct." This astonishing step made a lot of lawyers uneasy. *The New Law Journal* commented tartly: "It might not be unreasonable to suppose that one or two of the most vociferous critics of the conduct of this case may yet feel that there may be further revelations to come that may do themselves or their colleagues no real good."

The Bar Council came to the same conclusion and exonerated Muir Hunter. But the vigilant counsel had seen at first hand that if there is anything the Custodians dislike more than graft and corruption it is the energetic exposure of graft and corruption.

The most damning fact was not that the normal method of investigation, indictment, and trial had been bypassed, but that, without this almost accidental bankruptcy hearing, the Poulson network would probably have remained undetected. Some people wondered whether it wasn't just an isolated aberration. A less credulous view is that, if this had virtually fallen out of the cupboard because of mismanagement, how much more corruption is safely concealed by abler, more efficient and circumspect swindlers and fiddlers? Poulson is, after all, only a gentleman amateur. What about the pros?

An incidental irony is that, judged by the evident standards of contemporary British architecture, Poulson did good work. Even his most affronted competitors conceded that. Without resorting to any kind of leverage, and given clients with decent sensibility, Poulson's quality ought to have brought him plenty of work. So what pulled him off the tracks?

The explanation casts a long shadow over British provincial political and business life. Poulson opened his business in 1932. He was slowly accepted into an inbred caste, not so much a class nor even a formalized political grouping; Pontefract is a Labour town, but party is irrelevant when it comes to the transactions of men like Poulson. There was a brotherhood of interdependent businesses and interests. The doctrines of Westminster do not much concern the brotherhood.

There are obvious parallels, none of them quite adequate. The Mafia is one, but much too flamboyant. Another is the formal Freemasonry to which Poulson belonged. That was materially important, but not the whole story. No formal system with ritual and its own ranking, even though covert, is either subtle enough or pervasive enough. The Freemasonry was, if anything, *too* exclusive. The network that Poulson located and was able to exploit was not so much embodied in any one group of people. Nor was it ectoplasmic. It is a mutual but never articulated *ethic*. Local legislators and officials operate in a hazy ethical zone. The usual hospitalities and incentives of wining, dining, and freebies are impossible to regulate. The laws, so far as they exist, expect a court to distinguish where generosity stops and influence begins. It is a daunting judgment to attempt.

Among even simon-pure civil servants at the highest level, it is common for them to move, soon after retiring, into industrial posts where their experience is the main asset, not to mention a bag full of personal contacts. Inside such an essentially loose system, it is easy for the brotherhood of fiddlers to work freely without even brushing the letter of the law. The face of a man of probity is good enough, whether or not it is a mask.

The brotherhood did not sit on its hands when Poulson began to spill all over them. Money flowed in to satisfy the creditors. Poulson was lucky in having a brother-in-law prepared to walk behind and pick up the pieces, trying to salvage what was left. Maudling also helped out a bit, offering $1,250 to cover the design fees of a swimming pool he commissioned from Poulson. A labor-union official returned $1,688 donated by Poulson in the form of family vacations in Europe. Many others rallied to the cause.

On the other hand, the brotherhood was less helpful to the Scotland Yard men gathering evidence for the first prosecutions. They found that politicians and officials closed ranks, suffering either bouts of amnesia or sudden pressure of work.

In one respect, the brotherhood had grown more sophisticated. The art, craft, or inspired calling of public relations had many adherents at Westminster. Being thoroughly modern, both major parties employ PR men. Many M.P.'s, Labour and Tory, work for public-relations firms. Many a ministerial statement reeks of the glibness of the PR-washed mind. Edward Heath, no gifted wordsmith, retains an ad man for his most momentous sermons. And if anyone has robbed language of its meaning, Harold Wilson has bequeathed a whole decade of hype and anticlimax. Not surprising, then, that when the Poulson affair brought calls for a public register of M.P.'s' business connections there was a bipartisan resistance. Only the saintly molecule of the Liberal party registered their connections.

The generous-hearted Leonardo of Pontefract has left more on the British landscape than schools, shopping centers, hospitals, colleges, town halls, pithead baths, swimming pools, office blocks, houses, and apartments, not to mention a one-off swimming pool for Reginald Maudling. John Poulson, like "Tiny" Rowland and Sir Alex McDonald, is one of those men whose works are transcended by their implications. They are not the only ones, but each has significantly added to the picture of a country that professes a belief in one set of values while ardently pursuing another. Human frailties all, and by no means peculiar to the British. But the British aren't like that really, are they? If they are . . . well, *who* is left?

III. THE PATRIOTS

13. LOVE OF COUNTRY

Two Men of Their Time

The recognized reality of patriotism is not mere citizenship
. . . it is for better for worse, for richer for poorer, in
sickness and in health, in national growth and glory and in
national disgrace and decline. . . . It is not to travel in the
ship of state as a passenger but if need be to go down with
the ship.

—G. K. CHESTERTON

Somewhere in those fluvial bloodbaths where Angles
mingled with Saxons and gave a name to a mongrel race
there is supposed to be a spring of racial purity. Nobody
can quite place it. There is no shrine to mark it, no
Mount of Olives. The mists of folklore obligingly obscure
it. Perhaps it is not a time or a place at all, but something
felt in the bones, the seed of True Brit passed in the

genes from one generation to another. Its siren is patriotism.

Sooner or later, every would-be regenerator of British greatness falls back on appeals to patriotism, and it is usually a sign that things are bad. Pretension must end in reality; in Britain nothing postpones reality like an appeal to patriotism. Nobody thought it absurd that Harold Wilson, the token realist, should equate industrial revival with colonial piracy. It was done in the name of patriotism. Likewise, Edward Heath rationalized his obsession with megatheres by seeing it as some kind of virility test.

Patriotism is tangled with greatness, and greatness is tangled with ego. To defy this concept of greatness is to be unpatriotic, and to be unpatriotic is the ultimate crime in the eyes of True Brit. Whether it is the Hustler posing as the good patriot, or the bankrupting of the Treasury by trying to sustain a mythical value of sterling, or the pouring of public funds into "prestige" projects, the most suspect motives can be made plausible by draping them in a Union Jack.

But patriotism used in this way is a kind of incipient alcoholism. A little nip now and again to warm the belly does no harm, but it easily becomes addictive. It takes increasingly large doses to sustain euphoria. In some men True Brit has now reached this desperate stage; they represent a poisoning of patriotism. As their appeals to patriotism become more strident, they become increasingly intolerant of challenge. *They* become in their own minds the state. They know that in no other country can the "national interest" be invoked on more specious grounds, or so mutely respected. The mildest skeptic is, in their eyes, a traitor. Patriotism in this form, Super-Brit, serves as a repressive cover for anything from ministerial miscalculations ("Don't knock Britain") to deliberate deception. Patriotism has come to represent what the British *want* to see, rather than what is actually there.

Super-Brit is much like religious fanaticism: extremity of view born of a high sense of rectitude. The state takes the place of God, and if the state is Britain, the divinity is far from being rational.

PORTRAIT OF A PATRIOT (1): "SEEK NOT TO INQUIRE FOR WHOM THE BELL TOLLS"

Quintin McGarel Hogg, the second Lord Hailsham, is a muscular Christian. Fashions in political doctrine do not move him; if he has any recognizable and consistent strand of political faith, it is patriotism.

Until 1970 he was regarded as a distinguished lawyer who had sublimated a legal career for a political one. But he had served the Conservative party long and faithfully without satisfying either his own innermost ambitions or other people's early expectations. Then, just when he seemed over the hill, Edward Heath appointed him lord chancellor. It was a considerable consolation prize. Nobody more dissimilar to the new Tory philistines could be imagined than Hailsham, with his button-up boots, bicycle-riding, and fiery revivalist rhetoric.

Twice Hailsham had been frozen out of the Tories' higher councils; once by Churchill after he had attacked the great man's postwar policies, and again—more cruelly—by Macmillan, who gave him the derisory post of minister of science.

The complexity of Hailsham's Super-Brit showed at the time of Suez. As First Lord of the Admiralty under Eden, he was—like that other hyperpatriot Duncan Sandys—well in the Bulldog Drummond camp, keen to give the wogs a biffing. Nonetheless he was sensitive enough to discourage the shelling of Alexandria. But after the invasion was stopped, the U.N. enraged Hailsham by rejecting the help of the Royal Navy in clearing sunken hulks from the Suez Canal—it was a slight to British skills and pride.

When Macmillan succeeded Eden, it was Hailsham, as party chairman, who rallied the shattered spirits so effectively that, against all the predictions, Macmillan won the next election. But it was while he was helping this resurrection that Hailsham showed his clownish side. On the party platform he rang a handbell and chanted, "let us say to the Labour party, seek not to inquire for whom the bell tolls—it tolls for thee." And, as a sideshow, Hailsham made an annual ritual at party conferences of an early-morning swim in the freezing sea—with photographers at hand. Spartan exercise is not just exhibitionism, though. It is part of his philosophy.

Macmillan seems to have come to regret assigning Hailsham to a meaningless sinecure. In 1963, forced by illness to retire as prime minister, he favored for a few days the idea of Hailsham as his successor. In the public dogfight that then broke out over the leadership, Hailsham, on the brink of tears, declared himself ready to surrender his peerage if nominated. But another peer, ready to make the same sacrifice, forestalled him: Lord Home. Two years later, when Heath replaced the disastrous Home, it seemed that the thespian figure of Hailsham would disappear into limbo. Another generation had moved in.

On the grounds of academic record, Heath's decision to make Hailsham lord chancellor seemed just. The young Hogg made a brilliant start at Eton, and his performance at Oxford compared with that of Lord Birkenhead, a legendary advocate. He passed all his examinations with flying colors, became president of the Union (the debating society/club), and got an All Souls fellowship—just about the best equipment for either a legal or a political career that Britain can give its elite.

But the academic records miss the full flavor of Hailsham's youth. He was not just the son of a great lawyer but was raised in a pressure cooker of competitiveness with the sons of other great men. Randolph Churchill told the story of bibulous dinner parties where these sons would have to practice, under the critical gaze of their fathers, the art of public speaking. Birkenhead, Churchill, and the older Hailsham had political machismo; their heirs were expected to live by the same values. Perhaps that kind of pressure sat permanently on Hailsham's back. Whatever the reason, his evident talents were shadowed by nagging doubts as his public life progressed. They were ultimately the cause of his failure to win the party leadership, and they were entirely to do with his temperament.

When his father died in 1950, Hailsham's automatic succession to the title made tangible a dread he had spoken of since adolescence, the impossibility of a peer becoming prime minister. He wrote to Clement Attlee, the Labour prime minister, demanding a reform (made years later) to allow an heir to revert to commoner by choice. This letter was so rude and peremptory that even the crusty senior Tory, Lord Salisbury, was moved to call it "gratuitously insulting."

At various times since then Hailsham has gone bananas in private and in public, sometimes on television. He was the first member of Macmillan's cabinet to comment, on television, on the Profumo crisis: "A great party is not to be brought down because of a scandal by a woman of easy virtue and a proved liar." This caused the Labour M.P. George Wigg to say in the House of Commons later, "I would not pretend for one moment to be a Christian. If some of the ideas of Christianity which we have heard from Lord Hailsham are representative, then I confess that I am a pagan. . . ."

Macmillan, recalling private consultations over his own successor, has revealed his preference for either Iain Macleod (now dead) or Hailsham—"both men of great genius." But the cabinet demurred. "I think," said Macmillan, "many of our colleagues may have thought: well, they have genius, but in these very tricky, delicate, uncertain times we have to live in now, have they got enough judgment and balance?" For Hailsham this was the recurrent question.

Hailsham has a notoriously low boiling point in argument. He is easily goaded into petulant, arrogant, or emotional responses. Age has not mellowed him. He is a man driven by severe Calvinistic suspicions that moral and civil disorder are real threats to the state. His view of the Wilson years of the 1960s is doleful: he compares them to the state of the Weimar Republic and the French Third and Fourth Republics, and other countries "which one way or another have gone down before the blast of dictatorship." These views mark his public statements. As lord chancellor he did not withdraw into discretion. He developed a new, even more alarming vision of the assembled threats to the security of True Brit:

> In what direction are world events pointing? The war in Bangladesh, Cyprus, the Middle East, Black September, Black Power, Angry Brigade, the Kennedy murders, Northern Ireland, bombs in Whitehall and the Old Bailey, the Welsh Language Society, the massacre in the Sudan, the mugging in the Tube, gas strikes, hospital strikes, go slows, sit-ins, the Icelandic cod war . . .

Nobody else could quite so accurately have shown in one breath all the nightmares of the uneasy Custodian. No mention of Vietnam, but the Welsh Language Society . . . The enemy of democracy was, he said, indiscipline: "It is no use masking anarchy or indecisiveness under the bland names of liberalism or permissiveness." It was not "excessive authority" that was the greater threat, but "the frustration of government by dissident minorities." It was all suspiciously reminiscent of the Nixon White House. In other places and at other times, it was Reds under the bed.

Hailsham did help to define the demonology of the Custodians. He also gave an idea of why the lion had been so easily aroused by the flea. But how far was it really a collective paranoia, and how far his own private vision? No other member of the Heath cabinet was so wild in his language. Like Nixon, Hailsham was prepared to play on a simplistic notion of "law and order" as a political lever, although his version was called "liberty under the law."

These issues easily pervert language. As the campus polemicist will carelessly use "fascist," Hailsham uses "dictator" to include forms of separatism like Welsh nationalism. The implication is that "dictatorship" is a refusal to conform. In such a lexicon, dissent easily becomes a crime, the crime of refusing to accept that minorities should trust the state to look after their interests in its infinite compassion and wisdom. But in Britain the state—and the judiciary—have grown insensitive to minorities and do not offer equitable remedies.

Many lawyers outside the judiciary were unsettled by Hailsham's intemperate language and political engagement. They were also troubled by some of his appointments to the judges' bench. Although by nature and ethic lawyers are a discreet profession, they began to speak out. Lord Goodman, a solicitor and ubiquitous power broker, said of the *Oz* judgment:

> When a judge finds himself in the position of having to announce that he is not acquainted with the science of jurisprudence, and has never heard of the Professor of Jurisprudence at Oxford, there must be something wrong.

The courts reached their present condition under the supervision of Lord Hailsham. The lord chancellor makes the law-makers. He selects the judges. He is the one man in the country who sits at the confluence of the judiciary, the executive, the cabinet, and the ruling party. He is a politician, a lawyer, an administrator, and—hopefully—a man of impartial wisdom. An American president can, if helped by mortality, make the Supreme

Court his own. So can a lord chancellor seed the benches with judges who reflect his own sympathies. Over a few years the climate of English law can be effectively conditioned by the lord chancellor's appointments.

In Hailsham's case the appointments were, he admitted, a problem. "I am reaching the stage when I am finding it less easy to discover professional judges and magistrates of sufficient experience and quality." But one of his solutions seemed extreme—a curtailment of the right to opt for a jury trial. Only 2 percent of criminal cases go to a jury; the remainder are heard in magistrates' courts. Law administered by magistrates, most of them lay, has become disturbingly capricious, with anomalies explicable only by regional and personal quirks. Consequently more and more defendants are choosing to elect for jury trial, a trend that exacerbates the creaking court machinery. The need to remedy this was the justification that Hailsham cited for limiting access to jury trial. But his abolition of the right of the defense to know the occupation of jurors, executed without parliamentary debate, suggested that, like Sir Robert Mark, Hailsham regards juries as too fallible.

Hailsham's mark on the law has been that of a man with a driven sense of public duty, swept along by his own messianic convictions and the slogans of True Brit. His fervor increases as he senses that he is falling out of fashion. British democracy can be preserved, he calls, only by "a return to patriotism, loyalty, public spirit, and civic virtue." But then he adds that every time he has preached this creed he has been treated to "ridicule, unbelief, cynicism, and sometimes outright hostility." As Britain continued to bleed from its self-inflicted wounds, Hailsham had even more morbid premonitions. In a definitive speech at the end of 1973 he warned, "For the first time in very many years the rule of law is threatened, and threatened openly."

This time his target was the labor unions and their

parliamentary supporters. His definition of patriotism was, he said, "a man who put his party above himself, and his country above his party." And he added:

> Hitherto the British people have been great exponents of constitutionality, examples of which they are apt to call by rather homely names, like fair play, sportsmanship, what is or is not cricket, gentlemanly behaviour, tolerance or even just decency. It is at the heart of the British way of life and if it were lost, I believe the rule of law would fly out of the window with it.

Hailsham's definition of patriotism elevates the state to the position of a divinity, and then demands quiescent obedience to it. Those who don't share his own complacency about the decency and justice of the state become, in his dogma, a malign influence. It is then but a short step in logic to insist that the state is entitled to protect itself by repressing dissent. But the right to invoke patriotism and selflessness in the same breath requires a shared sense of equity, the kind of consensus that the British increasingly feel is ill-founded. It is this that makes Hailsham's "patriotism" obsolete, not the "anarchy" that he uses to label social grievances. But he, at least, has never confused patriotism with racial purity.

PORTRAIT OF A PATRIOT (2): LEADING THE NATION BACK TO ITS VALHALLA

In his Homburg hat and three-piece suits, the Right Honorable J. Enoch Powell is always armored in the unbending formality of the English gentry. Not one layer is shed on even the hottest of days, nor is there ever a sign of sweat. It is the glacial composure that used to be mandatory for British public figures but no longer is. Powell retains it as though indicating his contempt for modern laxities. It was the same when he served in the Egyptian

desert in World War II. While other officers—
Montgomery, notably—created their own idiosyncratic
battle dress, Powell appeared with his belts waxed and
brilliant, always the martinet and always the epitome of
the Indian Army officer.

But it is all a bit of a pose. He comes not from the
rural shires where Kipling blonds were reared and bred,
but from a lower-middle-class family in the industrial
Black Country of the Midlands, a background stamped
on his burred vowels. Social grooming has always
tempted him. In his desert days he had to spend several
days in a truck with a cavalry officer of high social rank.
Powell made a deal in which he spent the time instructing
his companion in Greek and Roman history, and in return he was given a detailed instruction on "the appur-
tenances of an English gentleman." Later, back in Britain,
Powell joined a fox hunt, going to the meets on the sub-
way.

Today the clipped military mustache is gray, and his
skin parchment white. Only the eyes, on the brink of
being hypnotic, betray the energy underneath. These are
not the makings of a popular idol. And yet Powell is the
one man who could make a new constituency in Britain
of right and left, rich and poor. "It is a subject," he says,
"which found me: I didn't go looking for it." The subject
is race, and he has made it his own.

Powell is more formidable as the apostle of racism
than anyone who has openly preached the creed all their
lives. He is replete with the credentials of a mature political career; he cannot be written off as a freak. Even
more—and this is something he relies on—he is always
characterized as a man of superior intellect. A translator
of Herodotus, scholarly, and acquainted with the richness
of Greek civilization. How could such sophistication be
aligned with a sentiment as crude as racism?

The belief in Powell's rigor of intellect survives some
remarkable inconsistencies:

OCTOBER, 1964: I have and always will set my face like flint against making any difference between one citizen and another on grounds of his origin.

NOVEMBER, 1968: The West Indian or Indian does not, by being born in England, become an Englishman. In law he becomes a United Kingdom citizen by birth; in fact he is a West Indian or Asian still.

None of the compounds making up the chemistry of Enoch Powell seemed either unstable or fissionary until April 20, 1968. The only fragile clue to some subterranean disturbance lay in his sense of Englishness. This surfaced briefly in a parliamentary debate in 1953. The empire was dissolving into the Commonwealth, and the House of Commons was dealing with the Royal Titles Bill. The nomenclature of the monarchy had to be adjusted to its reduced status. Powell's beloved Indian Army had gone, and with it the mantle of Kipling and the heritage of the savages redeemed by the white man. The young Elizabeth was only months away from that flux of national sentiment, the coronation. The spiritual levitation carried Powell away:

> Sometimes elements which are essential to the life, growth and existence of Britain seem for a time to be cast into shadow, and even destroyed. Yet in the past they have remained alive; they have survived; they have come to the surface again, and they have been the means of a great flowering which no one has suspected. It is because I believe that, in a sense, for a brief moment, *I represent and speak for an indispensable element in the British constitution,* that I have spoken.

Powell lamented the surrender of imperial power. Disembodied from the monarchy, his messianic rhetoric was hard enough to take. Directed as it was to the cause of the Hanoverian throne, it was ethnically ridiculous and historically fallible. The queen's blood is one part German, and her husband is a Greek immigrant. No matter. Powell's mind is gripped by a racial fantasy.

His perception of himself as the spokesman for an otherwise mute polity then sank out of sight for years, an ember waiting for a fresh breeze. On April 9, 1968, the Labour government introduced the Race Relations Bill, a first feeble attempt to legislate against discrimination. Eleven days later, in a speech at Birmingham, Powell reacted. The legislation was, he said, aimed at the wrong people:

> They have got it exactly diametrically wrong. The discrimination and the deprivation, the sense of alarm and resentment, lies not with the immigrant population but with those among whom they have come and are still coming.

Then, mixing the prospect of apocalypse with an emotive phrase of Blake's, he said:

> Time is running against us and them. With the lapse of a generation or so we shall at last have succeeded in reproducing in "England's green and pleasant land" the haunting tragedy of the United States.

But perhaps the most incendiary part of his speech was an anecdote about an old woman, supposedly living in Powell's constituency in Wolverhampton, in a street colonized by blacks until she was surrounded by them. To terrorize her into moving out, said Powell, the blacks had smashed her windows, she had been called a racist by "charming, wide-eyed, grinning pickaninnies," and, as a final gesture, shit had been stuffed through her mailbox.

Assiduous research after Powell's speech failed to substantiate either the story or the woman. Powell had carefully attributed them to "a correspondent in Northumberland"—a county remote from Powell's constituency. Powell later conceded that he had not himself checked back with the "correspondent" to authenticate the story.

Because of this speech, Edward Heath fired Powell from the Tory shadow cabinet. But political exile turned into political license. On his own, without further party constraints, he could serve as the catalyst for all the so far unchanneled racism. More important, Powell had done something that no leader of an extremist sect could have achieved: because of his status he had made respectable, overnight, opinions which until that moment were only whispered in the shadows of ignorance and fear.

As Powell developed his theme, becoming more cautious with anecdotes but more apocalyptic in his predictions, all manner of other pestilences came out from under rocks. Some were new in name and virulence, others were warmed-up versions of an old broth. Powell had made for himself a political constituency, but one that was sometimes unpalatable even to him. He took particular care to keep clear of overt fascists in quasi-military gear. Though a cynic might think otherwise, Powell's aversion to brown shirts was not feigned. He had not fought for Albion against Hitler, only a generation later to embrace fascism. To call him a fascist is too simplistic, showing the same carelessness with labels that afflicts a modern campus where the memories are unschooled. Powell didn't need the fascists; they needed him.

To the black Britons, perhaps even more than for their parents, the inequities of British life can be the source of something more violent than disenchantment. What are they to make, for example, of Powell's "final solution," that they should be persuaded to "go back" to countries they have never known? The shadow of Enoch Powell hangs over these people as the harbinger of an increasingly insecure future. Powellism's worst side is the tacit consent by which it flourishes, extending to the highest places. The more anonymous his admirers, the more influential they tend to be. Three millionaires, described as "major City and industrial leaders," embarked on a campaign to spread Powell's doctrine more effectively through the land. As always, Powell refused to be drawn into any overt alliance, content that these propagandists should do his work for him. Splendid isolation is his style.

Powell's speeches give fluency to the most primitive instincts of the inarticulate and barely literate. His first racist speech in 1968 produced an avalanche of mail. There were 100,000 letters in support, only 800 against; nothing was more instrumental in making this *his* issue. Of a representative sample of 3,400 of the letters, analyzed by independent scrutiny, only 71 could be classified as openly racist. By far the most common fear—1,128 of the sample—expressed the same kind of curious hyperpatriotism, the froth of True Brit, that Powell indulged in in his speech on the Royal Titles Bill. They were worried that "Englishness" was being undermined. "No Briton," said one, "wants to see his traditional way of living, the country he has loved and fought for, lose its identity, and particular character, through the over-great acceptance of too many peoples of quite different cultures and ways of life." More bluntly, another described the immigrants as "a non-British population which cares nothing for our traditions."

It may be unduly cautious not to brand these sentiments as racism. They reflect a morbid patriotism, the gripe of the dispossessed. It afflicts Powell himself and may even be the trigger of his bile. Those who know him in private moments say that, after a night in the House of Commons listening to the bleak managerial imperatives of his party leaders, he would slump disconsolately into a cab, shaking his head and muttering, "Our poor country." Marooned away from the decision-making and surrounded by admiring boors whom he despises, Powell has felt more and more like the only man who perceives his people's peril. It is the kind of isolation that can easily turn a man's head.

But Powell is not unhinged. He does not seek to create a master race of blue-eyed blonds. His England is for the mongrel English, as long as they are white. He seems unaware that it is the worst instincts of the English that he articulates, not the best. His has become the most divisive voice in the land, far more fundamental and arousing than conflicts of ideology. His only apparent solution is not healing but excision. And his own intolerance is sustained by a misplaced tolerance in others. He is isolated but not discredited, rebuked but not outlawed. Powell presents the ultimate and infinitely resistible dilemma of the democratic society: whether or not to tolerate the intolerable. In Britain the right of an urbane and erudite politician to put forward racist arguments is still thought essential to free debate, valued above the rights of a colored minority to themselves share the political processes. The benefit of the doubt has been generously extended to Powell. He has used up every inch of earlier respect and reputation. The only way of seeing him in the truest light is to be black.

Powell may well see himself as a kind of English de Gaulle, carried along as de Gaulle was by a surge of reactionary instincts which he secretly despises but which he is ready to use to propel himself into power. His hauteur, like de Gaulle's, rests on a higher sense of destiny. As did de Gaulle with Algeria, Powell has come to accept the loss of his once beloved India and even that "the British Empire always cost the people of these islands more than it was worth." He does not plan to appear at the head of a column of racist shopkeepers, and certainly not of a rabble. He is a man for All England, when it wakes up to reassert its independence and rediscover that spark in its genes. He is waiting for that, for then he will be called. He is the last patriot.

Powell feels that inside the Common Market, Britain

will disappear into a new European state "as one province along with others." He has offered this as the rubric of his ambition:

> Independence, the freedom of a self-governing nation, is in my estimation the highest political good, for which any disadvantage, if need be, and any sacrifice, are a cheap price. It is worth living for; it is worth fighting for; and it is worth dying for.

The truth may well be that Powell's adoption of the racist bandwagon is really a piece of opportunism, the first recruiting drive of a man collecting his legions under a false banner, keeping a grander strategy to himself. What does it matter if these legions are allowed a few skirmishes on the way, a few immigrants softened up? The army is still incomplete, but the first steps have been taken on the road toward that vision of an England in the hands once more of the English.

14. ULTRA-BRIT

The Long Backslide to Racism

The film is called *England, Whose England?* It sounds as though it might be some flight of pastoral fancy by Alfred, Lord Tennyson. But it is no whimsy. The faces of the people who pack meeting halls to see it are embittered. They are people who fear a nightmare that the film brings to life.

It is made in the manner of a documentary, slick and urgent. There are long-focus shots that foreshorten perspective so that a street of people seems like a compressed mass. In these street scenes many of the faces are black. The commentary runs: "Immigrant families move in, whites move out. The Asians take trade away from white shops, and the white shops close down. Asian traders don't make any genuine contribution to the community as a whole. They remit forty million pounds a year to their home countries. (*Pause.*) White women have trouble getting hospital beds. . . ."

England, Whose England? is an insidious exercise in racial poison, but it tours the meeting-hall circuit untroubled. No law restrains this kind of propaganda.

Another scene is in Bradford, a city with a large Asian population. Bradford's business is wool, the making of many fine cloths. The county emblem is the White Rose. In this film a man says, "It's a long time since the White Rose flowered in these streets." (*Cutaway shot to Asians.*) A woman says, "Our poor lads are fighting in Ireland while our own country is being invaded." And winding to its apocalyptic climax, the commentary says, "It is the fifty-ninth minute of the eleventh hour. (*Pause.*) To discriminate does not mean to hate but to choose."

Applause.

The twisted semantics of the final slogan are the hallmark of the Monday Club, the most extreme faction connected to the Conservative party, and sponsors of the film. *England, Whose England?* shows how much license is given in Britain to inflammatory racism, so long as it comes from whites. In the shades from gray to black that are the spectrum of the ultra-Right in Britain, the Monday Club is on the lighter fringe. Its importance is as a link in a chain. On one side the Monday Club connects with the parliamentary Tories and even with Tory ministers; on the other, a more blurred edge, it leads directly to groups that were once dismissed as a lunatic fringe, but that now look more substantial.

A seam of fascism runs through modern British politics, part underground and part visible. It has always seemed unstable: waxing, waning, mutating. But it is always there and cannot be underrated. Like any extreme, Ultra-Brit may at times seem comic, but it is no joke. It is judged best by the issues on which it makes a stand.

Before World War I there was a strain of extreme and cranky nationalism that pursued the phantom of an international conspiracy of Jewish financiers. Englishness was threatened by their manipulations, or so the theory went. These propagandists included the Roman Catholic novelists and pamphleteers G. K. Chesterton and Hilaire Belloc. Bernard Shaw called them Chesterbelloc, like a two-headed monster. Behind their hysteria was a struggle between the old money and the new, the English gentry and the Edwardian plutocracy. It was also a kind of simple-minded anti-Semitism.

Between the wars this strain of anti-Semitism fused with the formal fascism of those Britons, and there were many, who fell under the spell of Mussolini and Hitler. This movement peaked in Oswald Moseley's British Union of Fascists and the Anglo-German Friendship League, which spilt over into the eccentric salon of Nancy, Lady Astor. Pressure from these sources reached the British cabinet even after war was declared against Hitler. A group of eight Tory peers blamed the war on Jewish-controlled newspapers and wanted to appease the Germans. Churchill sent them away with a flea in their ear, but the sentiment did not disappear. It lay dormant, like an incubating virus. Its next appearance was years later, and the cause was the fall of empire.

This might have been transitory, a doomed rear-guard action fought to the memory of Kipling and the music of Gilbert and Sullivan. But it was regenerated by the emergence of immigration as an issue. The catalyst of diehard colonialism was the League of Empire Loyalists, founded by A. K. Chesterton, a cousin of G.K. and formerly a founder of Mosley's Fascists. The league was little more than an hysterical gadfly buzzing about the rump of the Conservative party. In 1962 Chesterton's organizer in the Midlands, Colin Jordan, quit to form the British National Socialist Movement. At first it seemed a lame-duck rerun of Mosley, with Nazi uniforms and the old Nordic dream: "The only basis for Britain's future greatness is Aryan, predominantly Nordic blood. It is the first duty of the state to protect and improve this blood."

The state's reaction was to slap Jordan in jail for starting a paramilitary organization. His surviving *Ober-fuehrers* learned the lesson. They moved with less flamboyance and more purpose toward a new and clear-cut target, the immigrants. Like Powell after them, the Fascists told unauthenticated stories about old women being molested and terrorized by blacks. Like Powell, they invoked Blake's "green and pleasant land" and warned that 1984 would find a "mongrel Britain."

By 1966, four of the ultra groups, including the League of Empire Loyalists, merged into a new block called the National Front. Chesterton remained its ingenuous figurehead until 1971. Waking up finally to the monster he helped create, he confessed:

> I had had more than enough, after four years, of stamping out nonsense such as plots to set fire to synagogues. Two percent of the National Front are really evil men. . . .

The front developed political savvy. It acted as *agent provocateur* in volatile situations, especially racial conflicts. Anonymous thugs broke up political meetings with boot-stamping. And it was ready to catch the surge of feeling among the white *lumpen* proles that a black invasion was going to dispossess them of homes and jobs. National Front men went to Germany for reunions of ex-members of the S.S. The Germans endearingly called the front's new leader, John Tyndall, the *Fuehrer*. Tyndall aped Mosley in accent and style. But Mosley, skillfully rehabilitating his reputation as a political philosopher in Britain and the United States, dismissed the front as "dwarfs masquerading in the uniform of dead giants"—unconscious of his implied nostalgia.

With a formal membership of around ten thousand,

the National Front is British fascism without couth, a blunt and primitive instrument that catches the ugliest intemperance of the British character. It has been able to fan racism to the point where its candidates can collect up to 20 percent of the vote in both local and national elections in districts where immigrants are an issue. The front thrives in that seedbed of racism, the Midlands. Sometimes its proletarian roots extend up into the lower middle class, where it makes tentative contact with the Monday Club. There is no natural sympathy between them; the class gulf is too strong. But it can be expedient to connect the chain.

The front's support is visceral, and it is as popular with Labour voters as Tory. The Monday Club is an orbiting remnant of galactic implosions as the Tory party underwent reformation. Part of this debris is vestigial colonialism, supporting the white man's last stand in Africa. Another part is a semicoherent form of populism, resisting big business and big government. Yet another part is the familiar "law and order" lobby, which includes a hard line against students and labor unions. All this would be definable as the classical hard core of conservatism by any name, ancient laments and fashionable fears interwoven. But there is a putrefying additive, racism.

Without this, the Monday Club could claim, within the generous British conventions, to be "respectable." With it, all the other causes of True Brit are tarnished.

Six members of the first Heath administration belonged to the Monday Club and some, like Geoffrey Rippon, the British Common Market negotiator, had great influence. Thirty Tory M.P.'s were members. Few of them were closet Fascists, and as the racist fringe of the Monday Club gained a greater hold, the ministerial membership dwindled and twenty of the M.P.'s resigned. Nonetheless, it is significant that powerful Tories stayed in the club while it conducted some grotesque essays in racism like *England, Whose England?* Only the preservation of a political career, rather than revulsion at these tactics, thinned the ranks.

The most significant fact about the British Right is what is not there—a leader. The gray of the Monday Club, splitting itself into darker factions, and the black of the National Front are bridgeable, as were the *Waffen* S.S. and the old Junkers leadership of the German general staff. But there is, as yet, nobody able or willing to carry the torch. Powell, the apparent candidate, does not fit. Where he is an academic theoretician, the Monday Club is predominantly nonintellectual and petit-bourgeois, a rallying point for British Babbitts.

Leaderless or not, the ultras of the right can reflect with satisfaction that if you have a strong enough cause, you don't need a leader to get results. Ever since race surfaced as an issue in Britain, government legislators have adopted the technique of the steady moral backslide. Every pressure from the extreme right in the House of Commons, even at the beginning when it was represented only by cranks who were easily resisted on other issues, has been conceded. Successive governments, Conservative and Labour, have introduced progressively tighter controls on immigration and yet made only the most pathetic token measures against discrimination.

Bigots have been consistently appeased, while the blacks have been deflected from any credible political influence. The witch-hunting of immigrants has been legitimized. Both covert and open discrimination is unimpeded on a wide scale. And any refusal by the blacks passively to accept these terms causes, even among the liberals, hysterical appeals to resist "militancy." It is pretty obvious where the successful militancy is.

The shifting terms of British cant are encapsulated by a Jamaican:

In 1944 I was in the British Air Force fighting for freedom and democracy. In 1947 I became a settler in Nottingham.

In the 1958 race riots I became a colored man. In the 1962 Commonwealth Immigration Act I became a colored immigrant. And in 1968 I became an unwanted colored man.

It is hard to see British liberalism as anything but counterfeit. There is nothing in their records to distinguish the racial policies of the Conservative and Labour parties. For example, the Macmillan government of the early sixties was reckoned to be as left-wing as any Tory government dare be. Macmillan decolonized Africa at a rate that enraged his right wing. The socially reforming core of the government was led by the home secretary, the patrician R. A. Butler. And yet it was Butler who enacted the 1962 Immigration Act, limiting immigrants to thirty thousand a year and toughening the discretionary powers of the immigration authorities. Butler was the first victim of the right-wing backlash. He admits that it was one of the most bitterly fought episodes of his career. The lobby that forced his hand had its rump in the lower-middle-class Tories of the industrial Midlands. This is Powell's own major power base, but at that time he was dormant on the issue.

The racial folk prejudices are at their worst in this area. The populations are largely the descendants of nineteenth-century immigrations of Irish and Scots. It was a proletarian Tory candidate in the Midlands who ran in 1964 on the ticket "If you want a nigger for a neighbour, vote Labour." In 1965, when Harold Wilson first reversed Labour's race policy and continued the path of backsliding, it was pressure from this same area that provoked him. Labor not only tightened controls, having earlier promised to repeal them, but also endorsed the idea of "voluntary repatriation."

More legislation in 1968, 1971, and 1973 has all but closed the door to immigrants. There is now a bipartisan consensus upholding the line that began as the objective of a handful of right-wing extremists. In Nottingham, where the first (exaggerated) race riots took place in 1958, attitudes have been unchanged in fifteen years. A council housing official unconsciously catches the spirit of British policy: "People are prejudiced, and we must take their prejudice into account." He is trying to justify the situation where whites are given priority over blacks in slum clearance.

There are now about one and a half million colored people living in Britain—West Indians, Indians, Pakistanis, and Africans. Half a million of them are not immigrants. They were born British. And so it is galling for these British to see, as they often do, banners and posters saying "Send Them Home." They are home. Or for them to hear a politician of liberal pretensions talking of "repatriating" colored families. Or to see civil servants expediently inventing new categories of people like "Patrials," who are now the semi-British, no longer sharing the rights of the "pure" native stock.

Looked at through the eyes and experience of blacks, whether immigrants or British-born, Britain is a place with an elaborately organized pattern of subtle and blatant discrimination. For the young it is embittering:

> We've got nowhere to live—they shove the colored people in dirty stinking flats they moved whites out of long ago. We can't get work. I've got a cockney accent, so over the phone they say OK. But when you go for an interview, they say fill in this form and that's the last you hear of it. We get framed. One day I was walking along and a car pulled up and four detectives jumped out, they grabbed me, searched me. They found two medical tablets I had to take. Then they took me down to the station and said, "You're not leaving here till we find a charge." They researched me and "found" some more tablets I'd never seen before. All we can do now is resort to violence. You're still going to get done if you do nothing, so you might as well inflict some real damage.

The unemployment rate among black youths, like this one in a London inner suburb, is three times the national average. Black Britons leave school after being given the expectations of a white society, only to find that immediately the equality they felt and enjoyed at school no longer applies. The immigrants were lured to Britain for one purpose: to become a new proletariat, to do work that has become too menial, too arduous, or too dirty for white hands. From being subject races in the British colonies they are now subject races in the British domestic economy. They are indispensable and yet resented, an expedient resource and an ethnic irritation.

In a country with a long history of rinsing its conscience with words, the language is versatile in euphemisms. Even trained social workers unthinkingly use the term "host community" to describe the white population. The implication is that the blacks are there on sufferance, and as long as they abide by the conventions, rules, and desires of their "hosts" they can remain. If only they could, overnight, become white, there would be no problem. Here, for an example, as a typical piece of doublethink from the mouth of Roy Hattersley, a Labour politician regarded as liberal:

> We are all in favor of some sort of limitation on immigration. We all wholeheartedly oppose any sort of discrimination. We all wholeheartedly agree that there should be assimilation or adjustment, whichever word one prefers to use. . . .

All the "adjustments" have to be made by the blacks. And the dream of assimilation persists, as though the ethnic characteristics are offensive and must be surrendered as part of the price to be paid for enjoying life in this, the best of all possible worlds. It is not that the careless white phrases are really so appalling in themselves so much as that they support the illusion of tolerance and liberalism. The assumed magnanimity of the British used to masquerade under the image of the "Mother Country," that lady of empire whose children, of whatever color, were so welcome. It now seems that the Mother Country was the Fatherland in drag: there is a hardness in her eye and her heart that betrays a change of gender.

One of Enoch Powell's constant themes, from the 1968 speech onward, has been to suggest that British racial problems will follow the American pattern. It seems a specious analogy on the figures: Britain's colored population is barely 3 percent, compared to 11 percent in the United States. And since the British blacks are relative newcomers, they are not a group with a long history of suppressed civil rights. But these assumptions are deceptive. There are some striking historical similarities between the British and American policies on race.

The migrations of American blacks from the plantations of the South to the cities of the North is a paradigm of the migration of blacks from British colonial estates to the British industrial cities. The relative absence in Britain of a history of racial discrimination is more than compensated for by the endemic class discrimination, which mutates readily into ethnic discrimination. As with the American blacks when they arrived in the northern cities, the immigrants in Britain have been dumped where there are the worst housing and social conditions, cheek by jowl with an abused white proletariat, and depending on social services that cannot cope.

The attitude of white authority to British blacks also has striking echoes of what happened in the United States several generations ago. London's black population is now at about the same level as New York's during the great migration of 1910–20. In New York, Tammany Hall sought to handle the problem by creating the United Colored Democracy. The control lay with the white elites. Any blacks who failed to be placated by this arrangement were kicked out, stigmatized as "militants." The reaction of the British authorities has been identical. The most well-meaning effort has come from the voluntary initiatives of a traditional source of British social philanthropy, the Liberal paternalists. As they once did in trying to cope with the abject miseries of the working class, the Liberals have tried to neutralize the tension rather than offer real equality. During two decades of immigration, the blacks have been encouraged to exist in their own cocoon and discouraged from direct political intervention.

The result is that there are no national black political leaders in Westminster (or anyplace else); no black officials at senior levels in labor unions (or virtually at any level); no black managerial voices in industry; no blacks at any decisive level in the media (or virtually at any level); very few practicing black lawyers; and a derisory number of blacks in the police force. Wherever it counts, the blacks are unrepresented. They are as good as disenfranchised.

While the white liberals talk of "assimilation" and "adjustment," the blacks are being isolated into powerless groups outside all the conventional white decision-holding bodies. In Britain the Liberal Hour has run out of time, and it has achieved nothing. Its impotence is in grim contrast to the countervailing forces.

Britain would grind to a halt without its black proletariat. In its poorest-paid categories the hospital service depends on them. Black nurses and technicians are indispensable. Half the junior doctors are immigrants. This has gone beyond expediency to become an accepted role. And yet the same people who depend on services maintained by black labor are those who want to see the blacks "contained" as a pliant minority, or thrown out of the country.

Race-relations policy closely follows the pattern of British attitudes toward Northern Ireland. In both cases the normal civil rights of a substantial minority were withdrawn. In both cases the native talent for temporizing creates the illusion of remedy. The instinct for repression is more influential than the instinct for the supposed saintly national virtues. It is the extremist minority that is appeased, not those who are discriminated against. As with Northern Ireland, the pressure of smoldering resentment that this builds up is ineluctable. Britain has no special immunity to a racial disaster, however much the national conscience is paraded.

In 1685, 50,000 Huguenot refugees, driven from France by the persecutions of Louis XIV, settled in England. At first there was alarm that the immigrants were from an alien culture, and would be an economic threat. But, as a chronicler later conceded, "instead of doing us a hurt, it was soon discovered that they had proved a great and manifest blessing."

15. PUBLIC LIFE AND PRIVATE PASSIONS

Letting It All Hang Out

At first she hit Miss G. with a plastic belt. Then Mr. Z. and Miss G. tied her to the bed, and after Miss G. had left, Mr. Z. hit her with his hand on her bottom.

—MISS L., WITNESS IN A LONDON COURT

What's going on here? Somebody is having some fun; somebody has been caught having some fun; somebody is being made to suffer for having that fun (though not by the use of a plastic belt); some people are going to get away with it, since they have been granted alphabetical anonymity. Here are the basic ingredients of the British way of sex: flagellation, bondage, ass worship, and institutional reprisal.

There is no statistical proof that the British are more sexually resourceful than the Germans, French, or Japanese. There is evidence that the British public-school system encourages buggery, but not that it invented it. The French may believe, as they apparently do, that flagellation is *la vice anglaise*. But this may be nothing better than a cherished stereotype. The British have, in any case, come to suspect that the French libido is an exaggeration. After decades of believing in naughty Paris, the British now regard it as a Puritan backwater.

The curiosity of the British way of sex lies not in its technical quality but in the social and political attitudes attached to it. The same flame licks the loins of the British as of anyone else, but somewhere between the erogenous zones and the head funny things start to happen.

> Miss A. mentioned men connected with Kit-E-Kat, Silvikrin, and Smartie advertisements. Miss C. mentioned a breakfast cereal: "She said I was to dress in a school uniform, and I was told I was to be an eleven-year-old girl with reference to television adverts for things like Sugar Puffs."

Sex has not been a recent discovery in Britain, it has just gone public. It takes a lot of getting used to. The libertine life was once much more of a private activity. Privacy is very much a privilege; you have to be able to afford it. This meant that the rich and the powerful were the best concealed when they played games. And this created the misleading impression that they didn't play, at least not much.

The idea of sexual equality is as disturbing to the British ruling caste as the ideas of equality of wealth or opportunity. Moral superiority is an indispensable part of authority; if it goes, it becomes impossible for the powerful to impose moral sanctions on others. The more that the rulers are caught with their pants down in public, the more exposed is their cant. It is the worst kind of indignity, and as they are being caught more often they become ludicrous and more vengeful. Their fury is increased because, in going public, sex has been avidly taken up by the people.

> At Claridge's there must have been about twelve girls and approximately twelve men. There was sexual activity between all the men and all the girls. I was requested to fondle the girls' breasts.

Not just in Claridge's, but all over London you can see the smile of knowingness. Sex in Britain has become *accessible*—which means more than available. The first requirement of accessibility is knowledge; if you know how to do it, why it is done, then you can expect to enjoy it. Enjoying it, the Victorian sin, is much easier now. And that is precisely what makes the Puritans mad.

The Puritan backlash—it might almost be another sexual innovation—has surfaced under strange leadership, the union of an ex-schoolteacher and an eccentric Anglo-Irish peer. The result is a kind of moral Powellism.

It took Mrs. Mary Whitehouse about nine years to progress from a nobody to a busybody. In her blue-rinsed hair, winged glasses, and sensible shoes, Mrs. Whitehouse represents the kind of modesty that becomes tyrannical because of its persistence. She is the incarnation of the British matriarchy, driven by some menopausal paranoia into believing that, unless sex is stamped out, lost virginity will bring down the nation. Sexual ignorance was upheld by the Victorians by calling it "mystery," something dark between the sheets forever mute. Mrs. Whitehouse subscribes to the Mystery of Sex.

Her own parents thought it so private a subject that they never discussed it with her in any explicit way—a situation that for all the progress since made is probably still fairly common. "You must be careful," they said to her, enigmatically. They relied on their daughter's capacity for self-instruction: "Growing up as I did in the twenties, as part of a generation which found no difficulty in talking about sex—though by no means obsessed by it—I gradually accumulated understanding and, I hope, responsibility. By the time I was grown up, the sense of 'naughtiness' had gone but not, I'm happy to say, the mystery."

One reason why Mary Whitehouse has become a formidable leader of the British morality police is that she looks so believable and so ordinary, an anti-intellectual when so many of the libertines come across as members of a patronizing and depraved intelligentsia. Another reason is that she has picked her targets shrewdly.

Her earliest and major successes were at the expense of the BBC. Over the years she has portrayed the BBC television service as an intruding philanderer, corrupting the innocent with its worldly humors, its lascivious dramas, and its impertinent treatment of authority. At first the BBC made the fatal error of ignoring her. But inch by inch, through subtle psychological propaganda, she unnerved the BBC leadership and wrung humiliating concessions from them. Now she hovers over the network, backed by an army of harridans, breaking the balls of anyone incautious enough to offend them.

The BBC has become so unraveled that it proclaimed a new program code to placate its critics. In the course of this it apologized for a scene in the acclaimed historical series *Elizabeth R* in which a naked girl was seen "leaving the bed of the King of France." The author of the episode responded brusquely that the girl had been in bed with the Duke of Alençon, "not the King of France, who would have been more likely to have been in bed with a small boy." If the BBC can't tell the difference between a satyr and a pederast, it is really in trouble.

When I arrived she gave me three whips; one was like a dog lead, leather. There was another one, brown leather, sort of plaited. There was another; it was an ordinary belt, with a buckle. And there was a piece of rope as well. Miss G. whipped Mr. Z. with a belt he produced. I was clothed and he was partially clothed and afterwards he handed me about £ 30.

For Frank, Lord Longford, the point on the road to the sexual Damascus was a performance of *Oh! Calcutta!* He walked out halfway through: "It was only intended to shock with sexual display . . . when I realized that it couldn't be prosecuted, I suddenly felt we were in danger of seeing all the defenses against obscenity washed away." This reaction set Longford on a course that has earned him the dubious crown of anti-pornographer royal (Kenneth Tynan is the pornographer royal). Like Whitehouse, Longford converts private phantoms into public threats. After his conversion, he went straight to the hardest of hard cores, Denmark.

Denmark now plays a part in the British libido that was once, in grander days, filled by Port Said. The gymnastic Arab pornography, with its predilection for sodomy, has given way in popularity to nubile Nordic inventions. Danish hard core comes under plain cover into numerous British suburban bowers, and Danish sex manuals, books, magazines, and movies pour into the warehouses of British pornographers.

Longford went to study the phenomenon first hand, as it were, only to be embarrassed on his return when the Customs opened his bags and found them bulging with fruity literature. He explained that it was all research material for a massive study on porn, for which he had recruited a committee of fifty. Longford is a wacky figure: the high, bald dome like Queen Elizabeth's death mask, rather ragged appearance, nervous jerky mannerisms, and a fluty, lisping upper-class voice. Old Etonian, once a Tory, then a Socialist, once a Protestant, then a Catholic, a don, an Irish patriot, banker, publisher, and inveterate do-gooder, he is engagingly self-mocking and eminently mockable. His antisexual crusade is his most unhinged act, out of key with a private penchant for spicy gossip.

When the Longford Report appeared, it looked more like a pulp novel, with the word PORNOGRAPHY in 2¼-inch red capitals on the cover. At the press conference to launch it, Longford and Mary Whitehouse ran into Xaviera Hollander, the Happy Hooker, cashing in on the occasion to push her own memoirs. Carnality met chastity, and they smiled decorously at each other. The report enjoyed a massive but brief attention, then rightly faded away. A few weeks later, when *Last Tango in Paris* opened in London, Longford was one of the first in line for tickets. "If you criticize pornography as I have done, you should be prepared to see what you criticize," he explained. Certainly nobody can claim that he is derelict in that.

> Mr. Justice Phillimore was trying a sodomy case and brooded greatly whether his judgment had been right. He went to consult Birkenhead. "Excuse me, My Lord, but could you tell me—what do you think one ought to give a man who allows himself to be buggered?" "Oh, thirty shillings or two pounds, anything you happen to have on you."
> —1920S OXFORD JOKE

Longford was at Oxford while that joke was current. So were many of the Custodians who now glower down from the benches of the law on the sexual carnival, their loins as dry as their wit. It is not so easy now for them to retain the composure of moral impeccability. Their cover has been blown. There was a diarist in their midst—the kind of man who didn't obey the code, a middle-class snob ingratiating himself into the elite to record their depravities. His name was Evelyn Waugh.

What Scott Fitzgerald did for the flappers, Waugh did simultaneously for the orgiastic British upper classes. *Vile Bodies* and *Decline and Fall* were celebrated as fiction. They were taken as satire and, in a way, not taken too seriously. You can always laugh at decadence so long as it is fictional. And as long as Waugh's world remained hermetically sealed in his lapidary prose, the cover remained secure. But forty years later, exposed by his diaries, the Oxford and Mayfair of the 1920s putrefied as readily as a mummy with its bandages ripped off. The truth was more bizarre than the "satire," and enough of the participants are still at large to require, for the sake of British libel laws, their names to be replaced by asterisks. The sex life revealed by Waugh was demanding and highly varied; the Bright Young Things never seemed quite sure of which sex they favored, or indeed represented.

The diarist's revelations were so instantly embarrassing that a group of Waugh's Oxford contemporaries, showing all the signs of the attrition of unstinted sensuality, convened to explain them away. They took the elitist line. So much, they said, for the idea that permissiveness was invented in the 1960s. It was there all along. But only for those who were refined enough to appreciate it. Like a good vintage champagne, sex was too good for vulgar and untrained appetites. And with this characteristic conceit, they slumped into postprandial comas, no doubt reliving the reverie of lost youth. But Waugh performed a posthumous service—he had caught the Custodians with their pants down.

> Last time I voted for the Tories, because they are my best clients.
> —MRS. NORMA LEVY, ONE-TIME BEDMATE OF LORD LAMBTON AND OTHERS

In a government somber with the work ethic, the Lords Lambton and Jellicoe were rare buds of life. After being caught in the embrace of the Tory-voting whore, both had to be sacrificed to the hypocrisy of the Morality Police. True, the engaging Tony Lambton once unwisely played moralist himself. In 1963 he wrote, "One cannot doubt that the harm this will do the Conservative party will be enormous," so putting the knife in for the fallen minister of war, John Profumo, whose private tastes

Lambton shared. Ten years later, caught by the "image-intensive" infra-red camera of the *News of the World* in the menage of Mrs. Levy, *à trois* and smoking pot, Lambton could ruefully reflect, "One of the frailties of human nature is that one can very often see things in other people which one cannot see in oneself."

One puzzle of this affair was: were the aristos the last ones left in London who didn't know that it was free? Or was there some perverse kick in paying for it, even when you knew your track record in seduction was dandy? Lambton's answer was disarming: "People sometimes like variety." And people sometimes like slumming.

But his answer was more convincing than the appalling self-righteous tone of the House of Commons when Lambton and Jellicoe were expelled from that club. It was that spinsterish meanness, the reprisal of the men who dare not on those who dare, in which the British like to indulge. And the episode provoked a typical essay in knee-jerk moralism by *The Times.* "The Protestant ethic," wrote the Catholic editor of *The Times,* "is not crumbling by sectors, it is the whole line of cliffs that is being eroded by the sea. . . . The traditional standards of British public life are under attack." But the traditional standards of British public life include graft, corruption, bribes, lies, exploitation, persecution, perversions, and a lustful pursuit by the rampant penis.

Nobody epitomizes the myth of Victorian rectitude more than Gladstone. Although he never strayed sexually, Victoria's favorite prime minister had a curious taste for the company of prostitutes, hoping to be able to redeem them with rhetoric. Gladstone knew well enough that British politics spoke with two voices, those of the public platform and the private pillow. He once said he had known eleven other prime ministers, and seven were adulterers. Two, the Duke of Wellington and Lord Palmerston, were among the regular clients of the brothel run by Harriette Wilson and her sisters Fanny and Amy.

Lloyd George was the last really randy prime minister. He had the morals of one of his native Welsh mountain goats. Excessively prurient, the Welsh are also noted for incest and bestiality, though David Lloyd George never had the need to improvise. "Love is all right, if you lose no time," he said. He lost little time and no opportunity. After him, British governments passed into the custody of men who were apparently too busy with affairs of state to try anything on the side. But the traditional cover of discretion protected the spicy lives of many of their juniors.

Lambton and Jellicoe were martyred for the pretense of a tradition that was fraudulent; like Profumo, they had to go because they were caught. Lords of the realm must not let the side down—but they can be let off lightly: Norma Levy, on trivial charges, was bailed only on the enormous sum of $25,000, another sign of the Stephen Ward scapegoat syndrome. It is not the British bedroom that is threatened by the rampant penis, but the British system.

The greatest sensitivity to sexual freedom is political, not moral. The salacious passages in Waugh's diaries were embarrassing because of the identity of the partipants, not the nature of the activity. Breaches of what was once a well-concealed private depravity behind the lives of public figures threaten the right of a charmed circle to continue its rule. There are attempts to write off these revelations as peculiar to the Bohemian Bloomsbury set. Nigel Nicolson's revelatory *Portrait of a Marriage,* containing the amours of his Sapphic mother and gay father, has extended the picture of Bloomsbury's ambisextrous confusion. But this was no isolated pocket of upper-class life, merely the least discreet and most voluble. And it was as hypocritical as the rest. Writers who piously censured Victorian humbug were themselves dependent on social double standards to conceal their own aberrations.

The British are not cock-shy, they are truth-shy.

Even now, the moral mythology of the Victorians is widely believed and assiduously protected. The British Museum still keeps under lock and key the full unexpurgated version of *My Secret Life* by "Walter," a devastating social and sexual insight into nineteenth-century middle- and upper-class life—although it is on open sale in the United States. "Walter" reveals a sexual callousness with which one class literally rode the backs of another. But he was able to rationalize this as charity: "As to servants, and women of the humbler class, they were proud of having a gentleman to cover them."

Sexual and economic subjection of women is ingrained into the British system. Traditionally women have occupied in Britain the place held by blacks in America. In the 1890s, at the peak of empire, there were two million women in domestic service. The domestic hierarchy of the middle-class Victorian home had subtle gradations of nurses and maids: head nurses, upper nurses, nurses, under nurses, nursemaids, ladies' maids, under ladies' maids, even stillroom maids. Over them all presided that molder of the formative years of the British upper classes, the nanny. She made about forty-five dollars a year and was the aristocrat of the serving women, often spending her whole life with a family, passing from one generation to the next. At every level under the nanny, male supremacy was built into the system: footman to maid; gardener to needlewoman; valet to chambermaid; page to kitchen maid; butler to housekeeper. And, of course, the master of the house to the lady.

Submission to male mastery, deference to male superiority, and the silent endurance of male infidelity are still bred into British manners, even though most of the servants have gone. With this weight pressing them down, British women are having a hard time getting out from under True Brit.

With women's rights becoming a party issue, even the most established women politicians are ambivalent.

They have been conditioned for so long to accept public life on the terms of men that they are often their own worst enemy. Dame Patricia Hornsby-Smith, a veteran rightist Tory politician, said during a debate on sexual discrimination, "This Bill will provide a bonanza of publicity for the extrovert members of women's lib, who will challenge all sorts of cock-eyed jobs in male professions to enhance their publicity." Baroness Sharp, the Custodian who skillfully neutralized male ministers, said, "The hard fact is that women have disabilities as employees. I cannot persuade myself that having got the right to equal pay, it is right that they should now ask that the law should see to it that they get the jobs, too." It seemed not to occur to Lady Sharp that any man with her abilities would probably have ended up running the country, not merely a junior ministry.

With backers like that, the bill to end discrimination hardly needed enemies. Nothing makes a male chauvinist feel better than a female Uncle Tom. The most avid opponents of women's rights in Britain are often the same men who want to send home the blacks, like the Ultra-Brit M.P. Ronald Bell, who says, "No one can seriously argue that we should not discriminate on the ground of sex. We rightly discriminate on the ground of sex in the whole of our social life. Discrimination is a good thing."

16. THE RECKONING

Everything unknown is taken as marvelous;
but now the limits of Britain are laid bare.

—TACITUS, A.D. 30

The ship sailed on, but it was a ship of fools. Occasionally
a troubled voice could be heard—nothing approaching
mutiny, and nothing that could not be rapidly stifled. But
one such voice came from a surprising source. In the
chart room the usual stately composure of Lord Rothschild gave way to agitation. Edward Heath's complacency
disturbed him. As Heath followed the monarch's lead
and went out to meet the people in a "walkabout," spas-
ticly shaking their hands and talking of a period of unri-
valed prosperity for Britain, the thinking man's baron in-

conveniently chose the same moment to reveal an alternative prediction.

On September 24, 1973, Rothschild was booked to address a seemingly innocuous gathering of agricultural scientists. Normally this would have been as electrifying as a lecture on the nutritional content of ground maize. But the press had been tipped off to expect something else, and they were not disappointed.

"Unless," he said, "we take a very strong pull at ourselves and give up the idea that we are one of the wealthiest, most influential and important countries in the world, in other words, that Queen Victoria is still reigning, we are likely to find ourselves in increasingly serious trouble."

This might not seem a novel view, or an unreasonable one. But there was more, and it was clear who it was aimed at: "There must be a major national change of orientation. We have to think twice about the desirability of courses of action which, in the distant past, were ours by right. We have to realize that we have neither the money nor the resources to do all those things we should like to do and so often we feel we have the right to do."

Only two months before, Heath had reacted angrily to criticism of his obsession with totems like the Concorde, a third London airport, and the Channel Tunnel. "As a nation," he told a meeting of Tory M.P.'s, "we should not falter in major projects which other countries take in their stride." But this was precisely the *folie de grandeur* that Rothschild felt could not be supported any longer. Curiously, the Concorde had been one of the first items put under the scrutiny of Rothschild's think tank, and it had survived the experience. Since then, the accumulation of other money-gobbling ventures had hardened Rothschild's line, and his views had become even bleaker after studying Dr. Hermann Kahn's report for the French, the one that had predicted that by 1985 Britain would be one of Europe's poorest nations. In fact, he repeated the Kahn thesis in his speech, predicting that in twelve years Britain would be half as rich as France and Germany, about on a par with Italy.

This provoked a backlash of hysterical True Brit in the newspapers; one dubbed him "Lord Doom." The new jingoists like Peter Walker were equally apoplectic.

But the background to the speech was even more intriguing. After Kahn's French study had been published, it was suggested that his Hudson Institute should be commissioned to do the same for Britain. At that time Rothschild rejected the idea; now, as a part of his U-turn, he was quoting the institute in public. Edmund Stillman, who directed the French survey for Kahn, said, "We regard the Rothschild speech as some measure of vindication." And he explained succinctly, "Social patterns, class patterns, and the use of social talent in Britain are more compatible with nineteenth-century production methods than the twentieth century."

Edward Heath, like Queen Victoria, was not amused. He summoned Rothschild and for half an hour heaped petulant fury on him. Although Rothschild was not asked to quit, the two men's relationship was never the same again. And Sir William Armstrong, as head of the civil service, delivered his own homily to Rothschild about the obligation of civil servants to keep their traps shut. Sitting where he was, at the heart of the Whitehall bunker, Rothschild had seen enough to blow the whistle. It was a thankless gesture.

As it happened, he was not to have to wait too long to see a situation that made his prophecies seem, if anything, rather mild. But in at least one respect Rothschild's assumptions had been as mistaken as Heath's. He had said, "The dangers we are facing require us to do something very difficult and which we seem to find harder than several other countries, that is, to have now the mentality we had during World War II."

It was a misplaced hope. What united the spirit and

purpose of the British then had been a common and clearly defined alien threat. In 1973 the country was divided amongst itself, flawed by the divisions of class and wealth, delinquent in behavior, and resentful of warnings. And so came the deluge. The day before the morale-boosting exercise of Princess Anne's wedding, on November 13, 1973, a set of disastrous foreign-trade figures precipitated a bear market in the City of London. Between then and mid-December the stock market plunged by 111 points, more than a quarter of its total value; propping up the pound cost the Bank of England $115 million, without any lasting effect, and fragile operations known politely as "fringe banks" collapsed overnight. The financial spasms were only a part of a confluence of pressures—the Arab oil actions, chronic inflation, and industrial disputes—which brought Britain to a peacetime crisis worse than most people had known in their lifetime. But, for twenty-four hours, the amnesia of the royal wedding was virtually complete; nothing displaced it. (Even by Christmas, when the macabre truth had dawned, the queen was still prattling on about nuptial joys in her annual national broadcast: "I am glad that my daughter's wedding gave such pleasure to so many people just at a time when the world was facing very serious problems." This was delivered from the comfortable insularity of Sandringham House, a sprawling rural retreat which, it was later revealed, was to be renovated at a cost of $800,000.)

The severity of the crisis was difficult to conceal, although its causes were more resistible. At first it seemed that the Arabs might make suitable scapegoats; they had, after all, had a long-standing role in the repertoire of alien stereotypes, ranging from the comic-postcard pornographers of Port Said to the semimystical desert wraiths that inspired the demented dreams of Lawrence of Arabia. This was not, however, expedient. Offense was not to be given. The Foreign Office Arabist lobby was suddenly restored to power. Desperate supplications were made to have Britain recognized as "Worthy Number Two Friend" (number one was perfidious France). An arsenal of British armaments was offered in exchange for Gulf crude; "to the British," one Israeli observed, "oil is thicker than blood." A *Punch* columnist was able to dress as a sheik and pass unchallenged to 10 Downing Street, where the door was opened deferentially. But the joker lost his nerve and gave up. Earlier, at the Stock Exchange, his reception had been more typically boorish. The jobbers, seeing a burnoose in the visitors' gallery, chanted "Out! Out!" and "Oil! Oil!"

Since the Arabs were to be placated rather than pilloried, where else could the blame be laid? By lucky timing, a more convenient specter appeared, one that would both be plausible and satisfy a weight of pent-up prejudice.

It was said at the time that the National Union of Mineworkers had chosen this moment to take industrial action because, coming on top of the oil crisis, its power to inflict damage was at its greatest. But then nobody involved in a negotiation seeks deliberately to negotiate from weakness. In this case it could equally be argued that, by moving when it did, the NUM offered itself too easily as an alibi for a paralyzed government and a deluded country.

To those patriots who had long nursed the conspiracy theory about the labor unions in general and the agitations of the working class in particular, it was time for the Reds under the bed again. It was not hard to give circumstantial support for such a charge. Rule Three in the NUM's rule book, composed during World War II, gives as one of the union's objectives: "to join with other organisations for the purpose of, and with a view to, the complete abolition of capitalism." Although this was vintage rhetoric from a time before British mines were put into national ownership, one of the NUM's ruling triumvirate in 1973 was a hard-line Communist. Mike McGahey, who started work as a fourteen-year-old pit boy in Scotland, was explicit: "Capitalism is an antiquated system that should be consigned to the dustbin of society, and a new society created." But, mindful of his audience, McGahey added, "That society will be created in our own British way, through the parliamentary system."

Out of the NUM's twenty-seven-man executive, six were Communists. This was enough to convince some people of a conspiracy. Lord Shawcross, once the attorney general in a Labour government who had sneered truculently at the Tories and said, "We are the masters now," but subsequently a right-wing convert, told the House of Lords that people were out to destroy the democratic way of life. A Lieutenant-Colonel Rose wrote to *The Times* from the bucolic sanctity of Devon to put the blame on a "minority of decadent intellectuals." But the most Draconian solution came in a sermon by the Reverend Andrew Hallidie-Smith, rector of an Essex village, who recommended that all union militants should be shot if they persisted in striking.

In truth, the dialectic of the Communists was a diversion. The moderates on the NUM executive outnumbered the Left (tallying Communists with other left-wingers) by sixteen to eleven. What characterized the whole NUM leadership was the determination of men not to be exploited as a cheap resource. A miner with a take-home pay of $77 a week was expected to be complaisant while the Arabs were asking, and getting, billions more for their oil. Put in more direct terms, the NUM was asking for something better than a raise of $17 a week for the man at the Rhondda coal face in Wales who said this: "If Ted Heath would come to our colliery, I would take him by the arm and show him how we work. We would go down the pit and walk two miles to the coal face, crouching because of the low roof. His eyes would sting with the dust and he would think his brain was coming loose with the noise of the drills. He would see us eat sandwiches with filthy hands and hear about roof falls and he would get tired just watching us dig coal for seven hours a day in all that din and muck. Then I would say, 'Would you do it—the stinkingest job in Britain—for thirty-one quid take-home?' And while he was pondering I would tell him the day of the cheap miner is over."

Needless to say, Heath never ventured anywhere near either the Rhondda or a pit face.

For a man manifestly deficient in imagination, like Heath, sooner or later his salvation will depend on imagination. But he was no more capable of understanding the real sentiments of the miners than he was of imagining the life they led. His responses were those of a monotonous programmed tape, repeating the rigidities of his pay policy and delivering homilies about the national interest. Even more characteristic of the man was the way he equated intransigence with courage. Never very far from the surface was the memory of his public humiliation at the hands of the miners eighteen months earlier, when a strike was ended by a wage settlement by independent arbitration well above his own declared preference.

To what extent Heath convinced himself that the miners were the sole cause of the country's collapse was hard to tell. What was clear was that many other people thought they were, even to the point of believing that if the miners' overtime ban were settled the promised security and comforts would return. The confrontation with the miners was an effective decoy action, for a while. It postponed further the self-questioning that ought to have been taking place. But not everybody joined in the deception.

Mr. Gordon Richardson was a troubled man. As governor of the Bank of England he knew the state of the books. Speaking in London to a group of international bankers, he pointed out that, even before the leap in oil prices, the country had been heading for a national deficit of more than $6 billion a year, a figure beyond all precedent and with staggering implications. There would, he warned, have to be "some years of relative austerity" lasting until perhaps 1984. To rub home this point, that day the pound sank to what was then its lowest-ever level against the dollar: $2.18.

But the man in the bunker at 10 Downing Street was still obsessed with the miners. The hawks in his cabinet wanted an election on the specious grounds of "who runs the country?"—a valid enough question in one sense, but not in the way they meant it. During the stresses of presiding over this embittered government, an intriguing change emerged in Heath's choice of lieutenants. Peter Walker, the euphoric hustler and champion of the fast-buck managers, fell suddenly from favor. He was one of the most vociferous supporters of the go-go economic policy that already lay in ruins, but his enthusiasm was unquenchable. It became an embarrassment. This was a moment that the Tory traditionalists in the cabinet had longed for. To them, Walker was more than a pain in the ass; he represented a nouveau-riche intrusion that went against the grain.

To Peter, the sixth Baron Carrington, the clipping of Walker's wings seemed appropriate award for years of dogged but not overinspired service. If you wanted to find somebody as the epitome of the English aristocrat who wears his arrogance lightly but unrepentantly, who is neither disturbingly clever nor gracelessly dull, Lord Carrington is straight from central casting. The credentials are faultless: Eton, Sandhurst, Grenadier Guards; membership of three of the most exclusive Tory clubs: the Turf, the Beefsteak, and Pratt's.

As Heath got into deep water, Carrington's presence—and it was *presence*—was more and more evident. The high and noble brow, the cool eyes behind the heavy horn-rims, the lofty nose, the wide mouth with just a curl of nastiness at the end of the lips, and the unmistakable

Etonian drawls of language . . . What had appeared, moving with assurance into a vacuum, was the father figure. The ingrained deference of Heath, the self-made man, had come out at last. It was extended, albeit with no loss of self-respect, to Lord Carrington. Here was a man of fiber, a man for the time, the rod for wilting backs.

Heath switched Carrington from the Defence Ministry to head a new Department of Energy, again the vogue solution to the vogue crisis. And, as chairman of the Conservative party, Carrington could combine the strategic with the tactical. Into the Energy Department went a formidable slice of Walker's empire at the Department of Trade and Industry, including the development of North Sea oil and nuclear energy. But one veteran of the North Sea oil and other policies did not join the new ministry. Sir Robert Marshall, in a dispute rare in its severity, had fought to impose gas rationing at the onset of the Arab action. Peter Walker had refused to follow this advice; Marshall was transferred to the Department of Environment.

Carrington was not the only emergent figure in the Tory leadership. The swing to the older values was reinforced by the new prominence of a man as apparently avuncular as Carrington was patrician: William—more usually Willie—Whitelaw. This rotund and bejowled figure had broken into the top rank of British politics as Heath's troubleshooter in Northern Ireland. In that tormented colony Whitelaw's diplomacy had gone down well; he had not sought to reconcile the irreconcilable, but he had found a wider middle ground of compromise than many had thought possible, isolating both extremes and creating at least a semblance of hope for the bridging of North and South. More significantly, in the semifeudal background of Ulster, Whitelaw had been able to bland things over with the manner of a patient proconsul; there was still enough deference there to suit this style. With

Ulster barely patched up, Health called Whitelaw home to take the hot seat of secretary of labor. His reputation in Ulster encouraged many people to feel that where Heath had been rigid and distant, the good squire Whitelaw would be more congenial and perhaps a mite more accommodating to the unions. If that was the idea, it died in its infancy.

Like Carrington, Whitelaw was an ex-guardsman, this time from the Scots Guards; unlike Carrington, he had been educated at Winchester and Trinity College, Cambridge, a soundly elitist training but less philistine. His club was the Carlton, *de rigueur* for Tory faithful but hardly in the same social bracket as Carrington's various retreats. It was, in fact, a perfect alignment of the squire and the aristo, one just comfortably below the other, their ranks delineated by time, a reassertion of class anchorage in a government that had strayed impulsively from such bearings. Heath now had a praetorian guard, either of whom might one day seize the crown.

Faced with the implacable miners, Whitelaw's previously unflagging bravura visibly wilted. Set in the middle of flesh-laden jaws, his narrow mouth became pursed like a blowfish at the point of maximum inhalation. He, too, seemed programmed by the same tapes, repeating the phrase "very considerable offer" to describe the limits of the government's bounty to the NUM. To Joe Gormley, the dour president of the NUM, the same message as before was merely coming through a rather more blustering larynx. The Whitelaw style had lost its magic.

There then occurred one of those inconvenient reminders of the social balance of the country that seemed to dog Heath. Whitelaw lists his vocation in *Who's Who* as "farmer and landowner." In Cumberland, on the Scottish border, Whitelaw was in possession of rich agricultural land. A few hundred miles to the south, Carrington's manor house in the lush vale of Aylesbury was surrounded by eight hundred acres of his own estate. At the time that both of them were engaged in defending the government against the rapacity of the miners, each was cashing in on the enormous inflation of land values, Whitelaw selling off chunks of his land at immense gain, and Carrington expecting $11 million for selling just 140 of his acres.

Heath went on national TV to tell the nation, "In the end our ability to survive, to beat inflation, depends on our willingness as a nation to act together and to act responsibly." This could appear only as pure cant when those around him were so actively feathering their own nests. Pushing the familiar line of the unrepentant authoritarian, Carrington complained, "Law, morality, every institution and tradition is now under attack from sophisticated people who have no constructive suggestion as to what should be put in their place."

The sense of impending apocalypse expressed itself in many ways. As the London Stock Exchange saw prices slide inexorably toward the floor of the 300 mark, sales in fine-art auctions broke the roof: Sotheby's reported a record $91 million in sales for the last quarter of 1973; a painting by an obscure Neapolitan artist, normally worth about $2,500, fetched $19,000—in pictures alone, Sotheby's had racked up $37 million. The consumption of exotic foods from Fortnum & Mason was unabated: smoked salmon, caviar, game pies, foie gras, and peaches in brandy enjoyed booming sales. But the spree reached all levels. Business in off-track betting, casinos, and bingo parlors was up nearly 40 percent. Other people chose more tangible means of escape: the Australian office in London reported that inquiries about migration had doubled. But the Australian minister for immigration, who happened to be in Britain, warned, "We don't want refugees but people who want to contribute towards building a new society."

Those too loyal to break and run were anxious to

show their patriotism. The sales of Union Jacks made a sudden jump.

Edward Heath did not concede that there was cause for alarm. Giving an interview to *The New York Times* in a room at 10 Downing Street chilled and shadowed by power cuts, he said, "We aren't in a state of continual crisis. I know anybody reading the American press will think this was the case because this is all that has been reported for the past few weeks. They have shown no interest in Britain for months and years, ever since the war; now all they do is describe Britain as being in a state of decay and of perpetual crisis, which does not bear any relationship to the facts." This churlish response showed how far the "special relationship" had wilted.

Heath's Panglossian view had been helped by a departure from Downing Street. The contrary nostrums of Lord Rothschild were no longer heard: he had been "ordered to rest" because of "overwork."

For more than two months Heath resisted any concession to the miners' claim. To conserve fuel stocks the country worked only three days a week, an astonishing self-inflicted injury to support a principle, immeasurably more costly than a settlement. But the issue was polarized between enforced adherence to statutory pay codes on one side and an increasingly bitter sense of grievance on the other. The NUM represented the worst-paid miners in Europe—worse even than in Spain. The status won for American miners by John L. Lewis a generation earlier was still denied in Britain. More sophisticated equipment at the coal face had done little to diminish the degradation of a job that remained closer to animal than human effort. Ironically, while he was confronting the glassy eyes of Edward Heath, Joe Gormley was told by doctors that he had pneumoconiosis, the coal-dust infection that is the legacy of most lives spent underground. Gormley's annual bout of bronchitis did not succumb to the bromides of Heath's pay policy. In fact, the so-called negotiations were notable for the absence of the craft of negotiation. Without an independent conciliator, the collision of two inimical attitudes was disastrous.

Finally, the disenchantment of the miners expressed itself in an unprecedented 81 percent strike vote, in an 86 percent ballot. Attempts to label this as extremism were sophistry: moderates had been converted, en masse, to militants by the kind of incomprehension that comes from remoteness.

Not only Heath was remote from the coal face. It required superlative feats of the imagination by anybody who had never been down a mine to contemplate a working life spent in one. There was a rush of reporters down the shafts to portray the experience. But as vivid as some of these stories were, the cold print somehow filtered out the visceral. It was possible to imagine the experience, but not to *feel* it, and certainly not to know how deleterious and unrelenting mining was as a career. The confrontation with the miners should have shown how, as in other ways, Britain attempted to support the blandness of bureaucratic dogmas like Heath's on the backs of people still expected to sell their services cheaply. The paradox of a miner being paid less than $80 a week while his seventeen-year-old daughter could make $100 a week as a typist was enshrined into the British value system.

On this issue—or ostensibly on the grounds of who should resolve it, the government or the miners—Heath chose to hold an election. Emotive words were attached to it, the bogymen assembled: "militants," "extremists," and the great Communist conspiracy. McGahey had said in a meeting at Downing Street, according to Heath, "What he wanted to do was to bring down this government and then to have a left-wing Labour government which he then believes will be pliable in their hands and their influence and the influence of their like in the union, and then dispose of that."

Whether or not McGahey was being disingenuous in

his caveat about seeking change "by democratic means," it was pure McCarthyism on Heath's part to brand the whole NUM action as a Red plot. (The total Communist vote in 1970 was 38,431—0.1 percent of the electorate.) But it was expedient enough to rally his party's paranoia, and to conveniently obscure the real crisis. It was a divisive course to choose in a country with a heritage of class division, and with many still unvented frustrations in its gut. After four years of Heath the average worker was about 20 percent worse off than a year earlier; company profits were up 16 percent and dividend payments up by 29 percent. This was the ground on which the government's obduracy was based.

Instead of winning a clear mandate for his policies, Heath sacrificed a working majority and produced a constitutional crisis. True to his peevish character, he did what no prime minister had attempted before and clung to power for four days, although defeated. The two-party system was paralyzed by an election result signaling "a plague on both your houses." And when Harold Wilson formed a minority government in Heath's place, it was another significant sign that events were overtaking a political apparatus that was more venerable than relevant.

There was the flagrant anomaly of the Liberal vote: they polled 6 million but got only 14 seats; the Tories, with fewer than twice the Liberal votes, got 296 seats. Proportional representation, a remedy for this denial of the public will, would have broken the hold of the two major parties and was for that reason anathema to them.

A deadlocked election was the appropriate culmination of years of delinquent government, and of the country's refusal to adapt. There was a sea change in the political mood, but one that was frustrated in its expression. One man who sensed this was Enoch Powell. He left in the middle of the last waltz, renouncing his parliamentary seat and his party. It seemed misjudged and even suicidal. But it was consistent with his private game plan, to seek noble exile while all around him collapsed and then to hope that the nation would recognize its true destiny in his hands.

The *Alice in Wonderland* quality reached fulfillment when it transpired that neither the election (called eighteen months before the deadline) nor the miners' strike that provoked it had been necessary. Statistics comparing the miners' pay with other groups had been miscalculated in Whitehall: the miners were entitled to a raise well beyond the limits on which Heath had made his last stand. It had been a contrived confrontation, with an ignominious ending that left the country even weaker—and yet still unwilling to concede how seriously it was flawed. In the hands of Harold Wilson, it was going to be *déjà-vu*.

In the truest sense, Britain is a deeply corrupted country. It is socially corrupted by the preference of class; it is politically corrupted by the retention of massive influence by a self-perpetuating elite; it is economically corrupted by a dependence on cheap labor.

In Britain, power, position, and success are still, all too often, allocated at birth. The more that patronage decides these things, the less is the opportunity for merit. In the United States, by contrast, the system is by tradition open and competitive. This difference is crucial. Americans don't accept that any situation, personal or otherwise, need be permanent. The British, on the other hand, feel with a depressing certainty that in many of the most decisive ways their lives are preordained. This helps to explain what John Maynard Keynes once called "a lack of animal spirits"—the seemingly blunted ambitions of people who have given up trying to buck the system.

Behind the survival of these arrangements there has been a resourceful deception. Things were supposed to be changing; the class structure was supposedly being dismantled. Proclamations to this end were frequently issued. Now, with the smokescreen finally thinning, it is clear that most things are exactly as they were. The reasons are intriguing.

Elitism is sustained primarily by the educational system, and by the endemic class prejudices of that system. To meet the increasing discontent provoked by the intransigence of this system, reform was directed not toward its dissolution but toward the construction of an alternative system. This "shadow" education service allowed far wider access to higher education and provided the semblance of democratic entry—*but it did not in any way challenge or erode the old preferential routes.*

Although the majority of British universities were founded since 1950, a half of them since 1960, this admits only the mounting pressure for the widening of opportunities. They have had a minimal effect on educational segregation. The number of children going to private schools has stayed more or less constant, and their social background is equally consistent. There are about 227,000 children in this conduit, 107,000 of them as boarders. Soaring fees are no deterrent: it now costs $2,500 a year to send a boy to Winchester (Eton and Harrow are a shade cheaper). Since there are supposed to be only about 100,000 people in Britain making $25,000 a year or more, the ability to support these fees is something of a mystery.

These schools have preserved their connections with the ancient universities, and these universities in their turn have kept their status as the recruiting agents for the ruling caste. The distinction of the two kinds of university is made tellingly in their names—"ancient" and "redbrick." The structural integrity of the elite is, as with so many things in Britain, equated with age; the precocity of democracy with an unweathered clay.

The calculated liaison between a socially selective educational system and the controlling hierarchies of most of the country's institutions is, at root, a means of self-preservation. The fact that it produces a vocational as well as a social bias should have made it seem more anachronistic than ever. Those continuing fiascos in Whitehall; the testy frustrations of the learned judges of the higher courts; the suave incompetence of the business managers—all these should have exposed the inaptness as well as the ineptness of the Custodians and their background. The continuity of the elitist breeding machine assumed continuity of role, but the roles were required to be different.

What lies behind this failure to synchronize the talent with the roles is the powerful emotional attachment not only to the continuity of power but to the world as the British imagine or desire it to be, and that means a world in which the supposed British airs and graces are valued above all else. There is a manic determination to sustain the ruling species in spite of everything. People who don't conform to this prototypical style—those who rate performance above appearance—are excluded from influence.

There was no murmur of this phenomenon in the 1974 election. Unlike the issues that did dominate the election, it is not ephemeral; it is not an infection wafted into the British air on an alien wind. It is permanent, resilient, and paramount. Why is it not faced?

Both the Labour and Conservative parties have adopted radical and reformist clothes, yet all their promises have been rendered nugatory. Each has been overwhelmed with economic crises; neither has seen beyond their immediate preoccupations to the real sickness. The country is locked into a repetitive spiral: governments are diverted from social correctives by recurrent crises without realizing that these crises have social rather than economic origins. As Hermann Kahn said, "With slow growth like yours, the rich get richer and the poor get poorer." The rich did get richer, and more of the poor got poorer.

Failure to recognize and reverse this process has built up dangerous stresses. Britain is far more vulnerable to incipient disorder than it imagines, and its complacency about its "institutional maturity" heightens its vulnerability. Edmund Stillman, the European director of Kahn's Hudson Institute, says, "British society is a great deal less stable than the British believe, and indeed there may be tensions—possibly revolutionary tensions—in the long run, which we're beginning to sense." He goes on to warn, "The British must not delude themselves that they are afflicted with a universal disease. It is not a universal disease."

It could be, as Russell Baker said in *The New York Times,* that the British are the wrong people to be running Britain. This made more sense than the hysteria of *The New Yorker,* which, as Britain passed into the eye of its latest hurricane, cried, "For the United States, the collapse of England, the nation that gave us our law, our language, and much of our moral tradition, would be a tragic event of immeasurable import." *The New Yorker* wanted a rerun of Marshall Aid, with "planes taking off, ships leaving ports."

This is the kind of absurdly romantic affection that simply helps the British feel that they are owed support on grounds of their superior sensibilities. It encourages the already pronounced tilt toward atavism, the mood encouraged by Enoch Powell that somewhere beyond the contemporary plagues they can find a Valhalla of empire where the rude values of the rest of the world can be ignored. Choosing this kind of cop-out would leave the driving and thrusting to the Americans, the Germans, the French, the Japanese, and anybody else interested in the fast buck. On these grounds decline might be acceptable, with the will broken and the dreams to live on.